"Progress is impossible without change. And those who cannot change their mind, can not change anything."

Dedicated to Pamela

For her loving and positive energy;
for bringing joy and happiness
to every person around her;
for making the world a better place.

ESTEEM
DISCOVER WHO YOU ARE

Mel Wayne

Mel Wayne
Author

With the vision of inspiring you to discover personal insights into who you truly are—immediately improving your life by allowing you to discover that change is possible—Mel Wayne presents his inspirational book, *Esteem: Discover Who You Are*.

The cure for all emotional diseases—anger, stress, depression, jealousy, substance abuse, greed, unhappiness, and discontentment—is presented in a new and enlightening way.

The Deluxe Illustrated Color Edition of Esteem is available!

Inspirational books, novels and games at:

www.FreedomWithinFoundation.org

www.MillenniumAdventures.com

www.TheGreatWayBook.com

www.Planet-Millennium.com

www.Gametasia.com

Visit Mel Wayne on:

YouTube   Facebook   Twitter

Cataloging In Publication Information

Wayne, Mel.

Esteem: Discover Who You Are / by Mel Wayne.

ISBN B&W Edition: 13: 978-0-9862942-8-0
ISBN Deluxe Color Edition: 13: 978-0-9642022-7-6
ISBN Ebook Edition: 13: 978-0-9642022-6-9

1. Self-Esteem 2. Self-Actualization 3. Spirituality.
4. Psychology 5. Self-Help I. Title.

Edited by Pamela Wayne

No part of this book may be reproduced by any mechanical, photographic, or electronic process, or in the form of a phonographic recording; nor may it be stored in a retrieval system, transmitted, or otherwise be copied for public or private use, other than for fair use as brief quotations embodied in articles and reviews, without prior written permission of the publisher.

The author of this book does not dispense medical advice or prescribe the use of any technique as a form of treatment for physical, emotional, or medical problems without the advice of a physician, either directly or indirectly. The intent of the author is only to offer information of a general nature to help you in your quest for emotional and spiritual well-being. In the event you use any of the information in this book for yourself, which is your constitutional right, the author and the publisher assume no responsibility for your actions.

First Edition. Printed in the United States of America.

Copyright © 2017 by Millennium Adventures™. All Rights Reserved
Copyright © 2017 by Freedom Within Foundation. All Rights Reserved

Table of Contents

Prologue	The Power of Thought	Page VIII
	Change Is Possible	Page 11
Chapter 1	Identify Low Self-Esteem	Page 15
Chapter 2	Recognize High Self-Esteem	Page 37
Chapter 3	Discover Others—Discover Self	Page 43
Chapter 4	Silence—Learn To Listen	Page 49
Chapter 5	Never Say "I" Until Asked	Page 59
Chapter 6	Eliminate Put Downs	Page 69
Chapter 7	Forgive and Forget	Page 79
Chapter 8	Live Life As A Leader	Page 92
Appendix	More Books and Novels	Page 112

"All things happen in perfect order"

- Prologue -
The Power of Thought

This book of esteem is about change. The only way to change is by experiencing an epiphany. The only way to experience an epiphany is by changing your thoughts. Changing your thoughts means changing that chatter in your head—that self-talk that creates your reality. Every person talks to themselves.

Listen. You can hear that voice in your head right now!

You average approximately one thought every second, that is about sixty thoughts per minute and 3,600 thoughts per hour. You average around 50,000+ thoughts per day.

Every waking moment, your thoughts are running wild. Unfortunately, the majority—over 90%—are negative thoughts. You are "programmed" or "hard-wired" for negativity. You have what is known as negativity bias. You have an inborn tendency to think negative thoughts more deeply than positive thoughts.

Before you learn to change your thoughts, it is important to learn that thoughts have tremendous power. They are more powerful than electricity. Thought vibrations are the greatest force in the universe. Thoughts are pure energy, lasting forever.

Forever is happening right now. All thoughts transmit an energy; this energy is known as thought force. Not just deep thoughts, all your thoughts. These include your inner dialogue, the constant voice in your head. From the center of your self, your inner being, a pulsating energy source transmits a signal throughout the universe. All humans have this inner signal. Not just humans, but everything, every physical thing.

All plants and animals and rocks and creatures in the universe emit a vibration of energy waves in a 360° circle.

The energy waves begin inside your body and move through space and time into the infinite universe and the energy keeps going, forever. Every single thought you have ever had never dies.

Thoughts are pure energy; they last forever. Once your thought energy leaves your body it begins its journey, outward into the vast universe, traveling forever.

Thoughts know no distance and never perish. Thoughts comprise the most irresistible living force in the universe. As living things, they have substance—shape, form and color.

Your thoughts travel faster than light. Light travels at 186,000 miles per second; however, thoughts travel in no time—infinite speed. Thoughts travel by ethereal vibrations.

Ether is the medium that transmits light, electricity and heat, among other things. Think of it as the air itself, the ether of space. Ether is also the medium through which your thoughts travel through space and time—like a glowing candle sending out ethereal vibrations of light and heat waves in all directions.

You are surrounded by a universal sea of thoughts. You absorb some, and reject some. Thoughts are transmitted from human to human, creating a universal World of Thought.

A tremendous power is generated from this interwoven matrix of energy vibrations throughout the universe. As you change your thoughts, the ethereal air around you also changes.

You affect everyone around you. The closer you are to another person's energy source, the greater the complexity of intertwined emotions. Your energy is measurable. It is physical. Other people feel your vibrations, right now. Imagine how complex and dynamic the energy grid becomes when more than two people gather in a group. Imagine all that inner energy, all those signals bouncing off each other. The air fills with incredible vibrations.

The exchange of energy is so complex that it continually affects all things, from two people, to an entire room, to the entire world, to the entire universe.

The energy waves become signals of attraction—like attracts like. This is the powerful Law of Attraction, in action.

The manifestation of your inner energy and thoughts create physical objects and directly changes events and circumstances. The energy exchange is in constant motion. It never stops. It is happening right now between you and every person around you.

Eight Ways to Change

1. Identify Low Self-Esteem
2. Recognize High Self-Esteem
3. Discover Others—Discover Self
4. Silence—Learn To Listen
5. Never Say "I" Until Asked
6. Eliminate Put Downs
7. Forgive and Forget
8. Live Life as a Leader

"Thoughts are the most powerful force in the universe."

Change Is Possible

All things happen in perfect order. The arrival of this book in your life is no exception. You are about to experience a life-changing event, an epiphany of the highest order. You will soon discover that you *do* have control of your life, that change is possible.

Your quest for inner change begins with an intriguing question. The question is, "What devastating *Emotional Virus* has infected human thought throughout recorded history, since the dawn of social awareness?"

The awakening answer is: low self-esteem.

You are about to discover that many people you know and love suffer from the emotionally crippling disease (dis-ease) known as low self-esteem, low self-worth, low self-image. Often referred to as "egotistical behavior", the *Emotional Virus* has been unintentionally passed from parents to children, generation to generation, since the beginning of civilization. All humans suffer from some form of low self-image.

If you doubt the above statement, think for a moment. Whenever low self-esteem is mentioned, the typical response is, "I don't have low self-esteem!" The reason people deny it is because they have it and do not know it. Low self-esteem sufferers are not aware of their condition, or they live in denial.

Whenever high self-esteem is mentioned, people exclaim, without hesitation, "Oh, I have high self-esteem!" As you will soon discover during your search for happiness and contentment, the people who possess a healthy self-image never make such statements.

Your quest to discover who you truly are has begun. There is an excellent chance you are already experiencing anxiety, denial, confusion, or anger. After all, you just read that your friends, relatives, coworkers, and life partner—everyone—suffers from some form of an *Emotional Virus*. Right now, you might be thinking, "Do I, myself, have low self-esteem?" or possibly, "I know I don't have low self-esteem; this book was written for someone else." Or, perhaps you feel calm and reassured, realizing you have finally found the answer to *why* you are so unhappy.

Whatever your reaction, one thing is certain, your desire to become a better person—to change—has brought you to this unique moment in time, to this page in this book—*Esteem*.

Relax, breathe deeply, and begin the revelation of a lifetime—the self-discovery that you are about to change, that you are going to grow emotionally, that you are going to find contentment. For indeed, the bliss of eternity may be found in your own contentment.

To begin your quest for change, you must determine how you interact with people; that is, how you *behave* toward others. Based on your own self-image, there are two ways you deal with the people around you:

1. The low self-esteem way.
2. The high self-esteem way.

The low self-esteem way, also known as "taking the low road", is based on intimidation, manipulation, deception, extortion, arrogance, domination, selfishness, and greed.

One or more persons "win" while all others are "losers". You will soon discover why "taking the low road" is the behavior many people choose.

The high self-esteem way, "the high road", is based on the even exchange of what all persons, or parties, desire. The result is fair exchange, give and take, a workable solution, a consensus. Everyone feels satisfied with the results or the outcome. It is always a win-win-win situation.

Dealing with people by always taking "the high road"—living the highest truth—allows you to feel good about yourself. To like your Self is the foundation for your happiness. You must like your Self in order to know who you truly are. Once you truly know your Self, you acquire the most desirable trait anyone can possess, high self-esteem, and you live in a state of contentment. Bliss.

A LIFE~CHANGING CONCEPT

Emotional illness, often described as dysfunctional and egocentric behavior, is the result of suffering from low self-esteem, not the reverse. Stating, "I have low self-esteem because I am depressed" is incorrect. The correct statement is, "I am depressed because I *have* low self-esteem!" Therefore, by eliminating low self-esteem, you eliminate depression and all your other bad habits, addictions, and egotistical behaviors.

The elimination of low self-image will cure all personality disorders, including anger, impatience, violence, hatred, revenge, anxiety, loneliness, envy, jealousy, greed, racism, eating disorders, alcohol and drug abuse, dishonesty, guilt, and depression—just to name a few.

When humans acquire a higher self-image, violence and war will end. Hatred and jealousy will cease to exist. Societies will function in a state of peace and cooperation. A collective consciousness of positive thoughts—high self-esteem—provides the foundation for a society of loving, compassionate citizens.

DO I HAVE AN EMOTIONAL VIRUS?

How will you know if you suffer from low self-esteem? What are the signs that you have been infected with the *Emotional Virus,* known throughout the universe as the *Dark Essence?*

You must identify what low self-esteem **looks like** and **acts like.** You must recognize the disease symptoms. By identifying low self-esteem— egotistical behavior—you will know if you are infected with the *Emotional Virus,* and if the people around you are infected. To acquire freedom within, you must be able to identify all the low self-esteem behaviors and eliminate them, one by one, from your life. You must change your thinking.

Change your thinking means: eliminate negative thoughts and replace them with positive thoughts—affirmations. The reward is inner peace. Freedom within.

AN EPIPHANY

People describe an epiphany as "a bright light turning on inside their heads". Often described as the "ahha" moment, you will know this feeling when it happens.

Your transformation, your inner change, begins with an epiphany. The epiphany unlocks your mind to the possibility of change. Without an epiphany, change in your life will never happen.

A life-changing event is about to happen to *you*, an epiphany of the highest magnitude.

As you boldly begin your quest for personal freedom—freedom within—your willingness to change rewards you with life's greatest treasures. You are about to discover the highest truth—that change *is* possible.

"Keep in mind that each moment is special, that each experience has its own treasure. There is no one time more special than another."

Chapter 1
Identify Low Self-Esteem

The identification of symptoms of the *Emotional Virus*—low self-esteem and egotistical behavior—is the first and the most revealing change in your quest for a higher self-image. It is easy to identify low self-esteem characteristics by describing low self-esteem personality traits or egotistical behavior.

Prepare yourself for an emotional revelation—an awakening—an epiphany. There is an excellent chance you will discover some of your *own* character traits in the upcoming descriptions. You will either feel enlightened and experience a change of thought, or you will experience feelings of confusion and denial, becoming emotionally upset.

You are about to discover that nothing, no thing, is more powerful than the truth—the highest truth—being honest with yourself.

Symptoms of the *Emotional Virus*

The *Emotional Virus*—low self-esteem—has reached epidemic proportions. You will know this to be true by asking questions. The first question you might ask is, "How do I know this *Emotional Virus, The Dark Essence*, really exists?" The way to uncover the truth is to ask yourself simple questions about human behavior, about common personality traits.

Begin with the question, "Do I, or anyone I know, act or behave angry, impatient, hotheaded, sarcastic, jealous, violent, cruel, hateful, vain, greedy, unethical, immoral, rude, phony, dishonest, co-dependent, obnoxious, oversensitive, irresponsible, rebellious, moody, depressed, suicidal, revengeful, unforgiving, materialistic, or envious?"

If you answered "No" to the above questions, ask yourself,

"Do I, or anyone I know, ever make fun of others, laugh at others' mistakes, interrupt others, talk only about themselves, argue, constantly complain, scream at a spouse, yell at a child, make obscene gestures, intimidate others, tease others, dwell on the past, procrastinate, sulk, or suffer from fear of failure?"

If you are still answering "No", how about the question, "Is anyone I know a liar, gossip, poor listener, braggart, loudmouth, talkaholic, blabbermouth, flirt, cheater, thief, racist, supremacist, workaholic, spendthrift, perfectionist, gambler, drug user, alcoholic, food abuser, sore loser, sociopath, dare devil, party animal, or reclusive loner?"

If you are still answering "No" to the questions, perhaps your should pay attention to the Internet, blogs, magazines, or watch the nightly news. You will easily identify the following low self-esteem personalities: dictators, drug lords, terrorists, carjackers, serial killers, rapists, arsonists, rioters, shoplifters, con artists, slum lords, and corrupt politicians—to name a few.

After answering "No" to the questions, people reluctantly admit, "Well, maybe I *do* get a little impatient and yell at the kids...so what!" or "Maybe I'm guilty of taking home a pencil or paper clips from the office...big deal, it's only small stuff!" or "When I scream at other drivers on the freeway, I feel better... anyway, they usually deserve it."

You hear statements such as, "I am doing what my parents taught me and look how good I turned out!" or "So what if I get angry, or jealous, or depressed; it's normal to feel that way!"

The responses go on—and on—and on.

Many people conclude their comments by declaring, "Okay, I admit I have one or two personality traits mentioned on the list, but that doesn't mean I have low self-esteem."

Another typical response is, "I know low self-esteem people are dysfunctional and I'm not; therefore, I can't have low self-esteem."

Are these responses right or wrong?

As mentioned earlier, many people will not admit they suffer from low self-esteem. Some individuals are somewhat aware of their disorders, living in a self-denial mode, but the majority of people are simply unaware or uneducated about what low self-esteem really is—what the *Emotional Virus—The Dark Essence* looks and acts like.

So back to the question. When an individual admits to yelling at children and then adds, "But that doesn't mean I suffer from low self-esteem," is the individual right or wrong? Is the statement correct or incorrect?

To answer now would be untimely and inappropriate, for the path to personal freedom must be traveled cautiously.

First, you must find out exactly what low self-esteem acts like and behaves like so you may begin your self-esteem journey— your search for a higher self-image, allowing you to discover who you really are.

It is time for you to meet those familiar low self-esteem characters you encounter every day of your life—at home, at work, at play, and in personal relationships.

You will learn how they behave, before you learn why they behave as they do. Low self-esteem personalities are:

The Intimidator, The Impatient Hothead, The Power Fanatic, The Sarcastic Assassin, The Depressant, The Oversensitive Soul, The Coward, The Hypocrite Liar, The Compulsive Addict, The Co-Dependent, The Unfriendly Phony, The Procrastinator, The Miserable Miser, The Show Off Braggart, The Unethical Trickster, The Stressaholic, The Gossip Monger, The Talkaholic, The Spoiled Brat, The Conceited Looker, The Pessimist, The Prankster, The Arguing Sorehead, The Unforgiving Avenger, The Unfaithful Lover, The Rebel Outlaw, The Moody Maniac , The Angry Bigot, and The Extractor.

The Intimidator

These *Controlling Characters* are the domineering physical *Bullies* who get in your face and resort to physical violence to get their way. Preying on smaller and weaker foe, these *Bullies* specialize in the physical threat, obscene gesture, or scare tactic before their opponent "gets the upper hand".

How do *Intimidators* function in society?

At home, *Pushy Individuals* are over-bearing and rule with an iron fist, unwilling to bend or compromise.

During school, *Bullies* choose off and intimidate everyone in the schoolyard.

At work, *Ruffians* order coworkers around. If they are the boss, these *Dominators* threaten employees with demotions and terminations as part of the daily work routine.

At play, *Brutes* wipe out their opponents, determined to beat their adversary at any cost.

At personal relationships, *Intimidators* rule the nest by harassing their timid partner into fear and emotional submission with violent threats followed by degrading put downs.

The Impatient Hothead

These *Volatile Characters* are angry and upset about everything, finding any excuse to yell and scream at family members, friends, relatives, coworkers and any unfortunate strangers who cross their path. These angry *Loudmouths* are incredibly short-tempered and easily provoked. They are extremely impatient, unwilling to wait for anything. They specialize in appearing calm but may explode into an uncontrollable rage without warning.

How do *Impatient Hotheads* function in society?

At home, *Yellers* are unpredictable and shout about the least little incident.

At work, *Screamers* recklessly raise their voices at coworkers, overreacting to mistakes.

At play, *Time Bombs* yell insults and obscenities, especially when they are losing or not getting their way.

At personal relationships, *Impatient Hotheads* cause their ill-at-ease partner to live in constant fear of being harassed, yelled at and screamed at—a fearful, one-sided relationship of emotional unrest.

The Power Fanatic

These tyrannical *Slave Drivers* are obsessed with total power and control—craving money, cars and real estate at the expense of others. *Dictators* believe the oppression of people equals success. *Overachievers*, unable to enjoy accomplishments, set unrealistically high standards, resulting in their persistent need to prove themselves. Envious of others, the more they get—the more they want.

How do *Power Fanatics* function in society?

At home, *Perfectionists* demand having things done their way, and only <u>their</u> way.

At work, *Controllers* bark orders and call the shots, methodically plotting the overthrow of others to gain position and wealth—power.

At play, *Tyrants* are too serious, becoming emotionally devastated when losing.

At personal relationships, *Power Fanatics* relentlessly pursue their "prey" and once captured, their tormented partner is treated (mistreated) as a worldly possession—object.

The Sarcastic Assassin

These *Put Down Artists* hurt your feelings. *Bad Mouthers* avoid physical confrontations, making you feel small and embarrassing you before you become a threat. Disguising cruel comments as friendly jokes and sarcastic statements, they complete each personal assault—put down—with, "Just Kidding!"

How do *Sarcastic Assassins* function in society?

At home, *Ridiculers* make one put down after the other.

No one escapes their wrath.

At work, *Put Down Specialists* are verbally brutal, making others feel small or embarrassed, then, laughing it off as a joke.

At play, *Sultans of Smack* taunt and jeer opponents into total submission.

At personal relationships, *Sarcastic Assassins* are so busy making fun of everyone else, they rarely notice their neglected partner. These *Taunters* are living proof that the tongue *is* mightier than the sword.

The Depressant

These *Downcast Characters* look at life as hopeless. They look down-hearted, long-faced and miserable. Always sad, often suicidal, *Lethargics* barely make it through the day. When asked why they are depressed, these emotionally *Lost Souls* search for logical answers, mumbling, "I'm not sure," as they unhappily sigh.

How do *Depressants* function in society?

At home, sullen *Couch Potatoes* are often asleep, or staring endlessly at the television, or mindlessly surfing the Internet.

At work, *Poker Faces* appear bored and listless, getting little accomplished.

At play, *Losers* give up easily and when losing a game exclaim, "See, I always lose!"

At personal relationships, *Depressants* are filled with self-pity and endless complaints. Abuse of food, alcohol and drugs is often a source of psychological comfort. Functional relationships are impossible as the *Melancholic's* partner suffers from emotional neglect.

The Oversensitive Soul

These *Overcautious Characters* take things very personally. Each comment is considered a put down and every statement has a double meaning or hidden message. When you compliment them by saying their hair looks great, they are thinking "I know I must look terrible, they're really making fun of me!" These *Paranoids*, always on the defensive, are unwilling to accept any compliments.

How do *Oversensitive Souls* function in society?

At home, *Pathetics* act temperamental, hypersensitive and irreversibly irritable.

At work, *Thin Skins* overreact to their coworkers' comments or suggestions.

At play, *Overreactors* are quarrelsome, easily hurt and deeply sad when losing.

At personal relationships, *Oversensitive Souls* never open up or show their true feelings. They are shamefully suspicious and untrustworthy of their partner. Worst yet, *Head Cases* over-analyze every statement, making conversation virtually impossible.

The Coward

These *Easily Embarrassed Characters* are quiet, shy, and think by staying out of every person's way, they will be popular. *Cowards* avoid confrontations, allowing people to step all over them. Having every phobia imaginable, *Wussies* are afraid to try new things or meet new people. Fear is their greatest enemy. Their favorite saying is "I can't." "I don't want to."

How do *Cowards* function in society?

At home, which they seldom venture from, *Reclusives* are withdrawn, allowing others to step all over them—do whatever they please.

At work, brown-nosing *Yes People* are intimidated by others, will not make decisions and are victims of cruel office jokes, ridicule and harassment.

At play, *Bashful Loners* are unsociable and reluctant to get involved—join in the fun.

At personal relationships, *Shy Scaredy Cats* are timid, coy and lack confidence, expecting their partner to carry the emotional load.

The Hypocrite Liar

These *Deceiving Characters* are two-faced liars, fibbers and perjurers. *Sham Artists* have been untrue to themselves and others since childhood, graduating from little white lies to huge lies. By adulthood, *Deceivers* lie so much they forget where the lie ends and the truth begins. They believe their own lies.

How do *Hypocrite Liars* function in society?

At home, *Liars* fib from morning to night, and when caught, firmly deny each lie.

At work, *Fibsters* make coworkers uneasy and employees mistrustful, often destroying the integrity of the work place.

At play, *Poor Sports* lie through their teeth just to win. Cheating is always part of their game.

At personal relationships, *Hypocrite Liars* create such an unstable family atmosphere that their partner lives with frequent feelings of deceit and betrayal, all because smooth-tongued, lip-serving *Charlatans* are untrustworthy.

The Compulsive Addict

These *Compulsive Characters* are obsessive, self-indulgent and out of control. Whether their bad habit happens to be food, drugs, alcohol, cigarettes, gambling, shopping, or sex, these addicts do not know when to quit. *Self-Destructors* have no willpower and are psychologically dependent on self-pleasure and immediate gratification.

How do *Compulsive Addicts* function in society?

At home, *Addicts* are unstable and enslaved to the refrigerator, the television, the Internet, the bedroom, the bottle, or some other form of instant pleasure.

At work, *Abusive Selfaholics* are unproductive and uncooperative, lacking the fortitude or stability to focus on objectives.

At play, which they seem to be good at, *Self-Abusers* love to have unending fun, often at the expense of others.

At personal relationships, *Compulsive Addicts* are held captive by lifelong bad habits.

These *Craveaholics* have no time for their neglected partner, only their own obsessions.

The Co-Dependent

These *Manipulators* are dependent on the people around them, obsessed with controlling the other person's behavior. *Enablers* are the *Reactionary Caretakers* of society; that is, they either over react or under react to the dysfunctional behavior of others. *Overcommitters* feel bored or worthless without a crisis occurring or someone to help.

How do *Co-Dependents* function in society?

At home, *Busybodies* anticipate family member's needs, then react by helping, then feel victimized, used and unappreciated.

At work, *Control Freaks* dominate others and stick their nose where it does not belong.

At play, *Whiners* say "yes" when they really mean "no", disrupting the game.

At personal relationships, *Co-Dependents* fail to say what they mean and never mean what they say. *Sociopathic Martyrs* force advice on others, then become upset and resentful, eventually ending the dysfunctional self-pity cycle with, "I'm being used...why am I never appreciated? After all I've done!"

The Unfriendly Phony

These *Cruel Characters* are unsociable, unneighborly and inhospitable. When you say "hello" or "good morning" they pretend they did not hear you and look the other way. Appearing aloof and uppity, *Rude Ignorers* can be extremely mean and uncaring. However, *High and Mighties* become suddenly friendly around people they choose to like.

How do *Unfriendly Phonies* function in society?

At home, *Uppities* are cold and distant, outwardly ungrateful and snobbish when complemented by a family member.

At work, *Socialites* are uncooperative and not considered a team player.

At play, *Arrogants* form a clique of belligerent allies, rudely ignoring opponents.

At personal relationships, *Unfriendly Phonies* stay at an arms length, expecting their insulted partner to tolerate habitual rude and ungrateful behavior. *Stuck-Up Snobs* hurt everyone's feelings—everywhere they go.

The Procrastinator

These *Highly Unsuccessful Characters* are irresponsible, unambitious and lazy. They are often uneducated and make every excuse to stay that way. *Excusaholic Goof Offs* are society's social drop outs—totally afraid of success and always expecting failure.

How do *Procrastinators* function in society?

At home, *Dawdlers* mope around and stall projects, never finishing a task or project.

Schoolwork is considered taboo and totally avoided by *Underachievers*.

At work, if they even *have* a job, *Backsliders* are methodically tardy, faithfully ignoring their duties—barely getting by.

At play, perennial *Quitters* fall short of expectations and are appropriately labeled as *Losers*.

At personal relationships, *Underachieving Procrastinators* evade all responsibility. Postponing positive events, *Hesitaters* become an emotional goldbrick to their frustrated and discontented partner.

The Miserable Miser

These *Miserable Characters* are money-grubbing, penny-pinching, miserable *Tightwads*. They believe money is not everything; money is the only thing. *Scroogies*, greedy and extremely stingy, never share with others. Hoarding began in childhood when they tenaciously refused to share their toys.

How do *Miserable Misers* function in society?

At home, *Controller's* decisions revolve around finances. Money is king. Activities are discouraged or canceled because of cost.

At work, *Greedaholics* act suspicious, mistrustful and step on others for a pay raise. They join coworkers for lunch, but when the bill arrives they sadly moan, "Gee, I forgot my money!" while moths fly from their wallet.

At play, *Hoarders* are too serious about winning and are poor losers.

At personal relationships, *Miserable Misers* relentlessly remind their partner, "Stop spending my paycheck! We can't afford that! I'm not made of money!"

The Show Off Braggart

These *Exaggerators* tell you how great they are—how they have done it all. From early childhood, these *Loudmouths* desperately desire recognition, craving the spot light. Dreaming of stardom, these attention-seeking *Entertainers* love to act and put on a show.

How do *Show Off Braggarts* function in society?

At home, *Story Tellers* demand continual attention as they boast about past, present and future exploits of high adventure.

At work, *Braggadocios* tell tall tales and act outlandish, anything to feel superior—to outshine fellow employees.

At play, *Boasters* dwell on the past, bragging about their extraordinary athletic skills—how they "should have turned pro!"

At personal relationships, *Show Off Braggarts* proudly repeat, over and over and over again, their extraordinary feats of fearless heroism and dare-devil exploits, reminding each partner how lucky they are to hear such thrilling stories.

The Unethical Trickster

These *Corrupt Characters* are cheaters, thieves and social swindlers. Having observed unethical parents since childhood, these *Scam Artists* have no scruples. Lacking moral fiber, *Tricksters* forsake self-honesty and truth for dishonesty and deceit, showing total disregard for their fellow citizens.

How do *Unethical Tricksters* function in society?

At home, *Scoundrels* steal from family members and if caught, firmly deny it or somehow justify the unethical behavior.

At school, *Cheaters* copy homework and tests.

At work, *Kleptomaniacs* steal everything they can get their hands on—from small change to large amounts of money or goods. Sly, clever *Immoralites* never fail to cheat on their income taxes!

At play, they are *Dishonorable Opponents* and *Poor Sports*—victory at any cost.

At personal relationships, *Unethical Tricksters* have no morals—they cannot be trusted. *Pretenders* faithfully cheat behind their frustrated partner's back.

The Stressaholic

These *Psychotics* are ill-at-ease nervous wrecks, agonizing over the silliest little things. *Worriers* worry about worrying. Experiencing one anxiety attack after the other, *Neurotics* and *Agonizers* create their own self-perpetuating stress and perplexing problems when none existed in the first place.

How do *Stressaholics* function in society?

At home, *Irritables* are fussy, fidgety and always troubled. *Insomniacs* never sleep peacefully, when they *do* sleep.

At school, *Alarmists'* nervous behavior is unsettling and unpopular.

At work, *Uptights* worry about everything, are always on edge, creating one conflict after the other. *Workaholics* are counterproductive.

At play, *Fidgeties* appear tense and tortured, in a big hurry to finish.

At personal relationships, *Stressaholics* are frustrated and scatterbrained; hence, their love life is destroyed by their stressful lifestyle.

They never enjoy a moment's rest or relaxation to focus on their discouraged partner.

The Gossip Monger

These whispering *Eavesdroppers* talk behind your back, causing social chaos by criticizing everyone imaginable—family, friends, relatives, coworkers, bosses and strangers. *Busybodies* start vicious rumors and put others down to make themselves feel superior. They enjoy sensationalism. They thrive on other people's misery.

How do *Gossip Mongers* function in society?

At home, cackling *Chatterboxes* are glued to their cell phone—spreading rumors about a close friend to another close friend.

At work, *Back Stabbers* secretly socialize and, during meetings, openly criticize fellow employees (especially management) not present at the meetings.

At play, *Slanderers* would rather talk about others than join the fun.

At personal relationships, *Gossip Mongers* create an untrustworthy atmosphere, causing their partner to wonder if they are being talked about behind their back.

The Talkaholic

These *Non-Stop Talkers* specialize in one subject—themselves. They are extremely poor listeners, always interrupting and appearing bored while others talk. These *Gab Artists* are self-centered and once they begin talking about their favorite subject, their life story, they will not be quiet. All you ever hear from *Blabbermouths* is "I-I-I...I-Me-My...I-I-I" from morning to night. The moment another person begins talking, *Interrupters* dominate the conversation with their non-stop stories.

How do *Talkaholics* function in society?

At home, *Rumor Mongers* appear indifferent and closed-minded, only interested in talking about themselves.

At work, *Non-Listeners* talk out of turn, suffering from diarrhea of the mouth.

At play, *Chatterboxes* are more excited about self-talk than joining the activity. They are, after all, full of themselves.

At personal relationships, *Gabbers* are inattentive to the needs of their partner. *Talkaholics* are rude without realizing it.

The Spoiled Brat

These *Coddled Characters* are babied and overprotected. They have gone from spoiled rotten toddlers remembered as holy terrors, to teacher's pet in school, to out-of-control *Shopaholic* adults. If they do not get their way, *Pamperedholics* throw temper tantrums and nag until their objectives are met.

How do *Spoiled Brats* function in society?

At home, *Overindulgers* demand being waited on hand and foot, nagging until they get their way.

At work, stubborn *Mollycoddlers* expect others to do their work for them. Since childhood, *Spoon-Fed Brats* have been taught a sense of entitlement.

At play, *Panderers* pout and throw fits of anger if the game or event is not going just right—their way.

At personal relationships, *Spoiled Brats* are perpetually pampered by their partner or the relationship breaks down and eventually fails. Unfortunately, the relationship score is always: "Spoiled Brat ten, partner zero."

The Conceited Looker

These *Cocky Characters* believe that "looks are everything". Being handsome, great looking, sexy, seductive, ravishing and glamorous is a life-long obsession. Endlessly admiring themselves, narcissistic *Beautiholics* dream of winning the title of *Mr. Muscle* or *Miss Perfect Face*. These *Vainiacs* have breast augmentation, hair transplants and nose implants, believing cosmetic surgery can cure low self-image.

How do *Conceited Lookers* function in society?

At home, *Hotties* desperately ask, "How do I look?" spending hours in front of the mirror.

At work, *Narcissists* parade around seeking coworker approval. Mirrors are essential.

At play, *Charmers* peek out the corner of their eye to make sure everyone is admiring their good looks, their clothes, or their bulging muscles.

At personal relationships, *Conceited Lookers* become bored with one-on-one encounters, preferring groups, gatherings and large crowds so fans can appreciate their incredible beauty. These *Body Beautifuls* and *Flawless Faces* fear one enemy—aging.

The Pessimist

These cantankerous *Doomsdayers* have nothing good to say—every word is negative. They are never happy and blame everyone for their problems. Rarely smiling, *Grumps* only laugh at someone else's misfortune. These habitual *Hypochondriacs* bring everyone down with complaints of not feeling good, their back hurts, or they are coming down with some illness or chronic pain.

How do *Pessimists* function in society?

At home, faultfinding *Alarmists* are despondent, overcritical and impossible to please—always unhappy.

At work, griping *Cynics* criticize management and never trust their fellow employees. *Cranks* are controversial, argumentative and disruptive.

At play, *Spoil Sports* are self-centered and determined to ruin everyone's fun.

At personal relationships, *Complaining Pessimists* whine, gripe and nitpick everything imaginable. Their picked-on partner never does anything right.

The Prankster

These *Annoying Characters* constantly clown around, make faces, or relentlessly tease others. Since childhood, just for attention, these mischievous *Smart Alecks* persistently played practical jokes and enjoyed making others the laughingstocks of their own peer group. Unfortunately, *Teasers* act before they think, resulting in their horseplay endangering others, both physically and emotionally.

How do *Pranksters* function in society?

At home, *Exhibitionists* pull one childish prank after the other.

At work, *Jokesters* spend more time taunting and playing mind games than they do working. *Foolers* are extremely unproductive.

At play, *Pesky Clowns* are comedians. Everything is considered funny and nothing is taken seriously. They ruin the game.

At personal relationships, *Pranksters* act silly, nonsensical and take nothing seriously, leaving their bewildered partner feeling terribly alone, out of touch, completely ignored and emotionally frustrated.

The Arguing Sorehead

These *Know-It-Alls* are always right and never wrong—they are experts on all subjects. Just for fun, these arguing, irritable, bad tempered *Soreheads* initiate and promote controversy, look for altercations to "lock horns with everyone". Whatever the subject, *Agitators* find fault with other people's point of view, instigating a confrontation, a battle of wits—a war of words.

How do *Arguing Soreheads* function in society?

At home, *Disagreers* argue and clash with all family members, looking for a good old-fashioned argument—a fight.

At work, *Sour Pusses* bicker and argue with coworkers and never let down.

At play, *Poor Sports* start quarrels or belabor a point until their opponent gives in—surrenders.

At personal relationships, *Arguing Soreheads* only want to fight and argue, anything to prove their point. They love to antagonize, provoke and verbally beat down their partner, a sure formula for failure.

The Unforgiving Avenger

These *Vindictive Characters* have not learned to forgive others—to let go. They hold grudges. Getting even is part of their daily routine. Resentment, bitterness and animosity go perfectly with these *Revenger's* "eye for an eye—tooth for a tooth" philosophy. *Begrudgers* have an axe to grind, a bone to pick, or want to settle an old score.

How do *Unforgiving Avengers* function in society?

At home, *Avengers* are ungrateful and full of malice, reminding everyone of past mistakes.

At work, *Blamers* are relentlessly uncompromising and set in their ways. Never cross them or you will never hear the end of how you "did them wrong".

At play, *Grudge Holders* will not admit defeat, expressing hard feelings when losing.

At personal relationships, *Unforgiving Avengers* never forget their partner's prior mistakes. They love digging up dead issues, bringing up your past mistakes and then, "rubbing it in your face".

The Unfaithful Lover

These *Untrue Characters* display a wide range of behaviors: from jealous *Possessors*, to outgoing *Flirts*, to insecure mine-all-mine lovers. Because these *Loveaholics* have not learned to love themselves, they have incapable of loving others. In "love with love", *Hopeless Romantics* are easily overcome by infatuation, immediate gratification, or secret fantasies.

How do *Unfaithful Lovers* function in society?

At home, *Double Crossers* act overprotective from insecurity, completely distrustful from jealousy, or absolutely inattentive from apparent boredom or disinterest.

At work, *Traitors* are usually flirtatious, even to the point of being sexually harassing.

At play, *Envious Interrogators* require frequent physical contact, convinced sex is love and love is sex—low self-esteem love.

At personal relationships, *Unfaithful Lovers* are never satisfied with their partner's behavior. Jealousy, insecurity, mistrust, fear of abandonment and harassment cause emotional turmoil during the unstable relationship.

The Rebel Outlaw

As neglected children, these *Unnurtured Characters* discovered that by being naughty, they got attention. Soon, these young rebellious *Radicals* craved recognition so desperately that they joined gangs, cults and began hanging around the wrong crowd. Eventually, these emotionally abandoned children became *Criminals*, terrorizing neighborhoods, robbing banks, gang banging, selling drugs and creating social mayhem.

How do *Rebel Outlaws* function in society?

At home, if they have one, *Outcasts* are restless and bored, probably plotting their next robbery or carjacking.

At work, which they despise, *Rebels* never last long and are usually terminated, or they quit.

At play, *Desperados* make sure they win—anyway they can!

At personal relationships, *Rebel Outlaws* place personal issues or causes such as robberies, terrorism, riots, gang banging, and trouble making above the needs of their neglected and abused partner.

The Moody Maniac

These *Ill-Tempered Characters* are society's manic *Mood Swingers*. One minute these *Schizos* are happy, the next minute sad, then calm, then suddenly mad. One day they are laughing, the next day they are crying. Sometimes they are exciting, then mysteriously dying. These *Erratics* are totally unpredictable and, undoubtedly, difficult to be around.

How do *Moody Maniacs* function in society?

At home, *Indecisives* keep family members in a state of flux—guessing. Anxiety rules. Everyone is afraid to make a wrong move.

At work, *Unstables* are so inconsistent that productivity suffers, and if the boss is a *Moodiac*—watch out!

At play, *Morose Melancholics* are fickle and skittish, never fun to be around.

At personal relationships, *Moody Maniacs* keep their

anxious partners guessing and off-guard, displaying radical and frightening full-moon behavior—madness.

The Angry Bigot

These *Cruel Characters* live their lives with hatred. Having learned anger and bigotry in early childhood, *Masters of Misery* are racist, sexist, chauvinistic, closed-minded and specialize in bashing. Secretly suppressing their rage, these *Supremacists* complain of being persecuted by everyone around them.

How do *Angry Bigots* function in society?

At home, *Hateful Zealots* denounce all ethnic, religious and political groups not meeting their approval. *Bigots* blame specific ethnic groups for their own personal failures.

At work, *Extreme Radicals* hide their low self-esteem views, instigating and promoting racism, sexism and employee unrest.

At play, *Xenophobics* are angry and critical of other people not meeting their "standards".

At personal relationships, *Angry Bigots* spend so much energy on bashing and denouncing others that their lonely partner feels ignored and unimportant.

The Extractors

These *Dysfunctional Characters* suffer from multiple forms (two or more) of the low self-esteem diseases. In other words, a person may be an *Intimidating-Impatient-Complaining-Unforgiving-Moody Stressaholic*, or an *Oversensitive-Unfriendly-Unethical-Sarcastic Talkaholic*, or an *Arguing-Gossiping-Conceited-Lying Unfaithful Lover*.

The more egotistical a person is, the more low self-esteem behavioral traits a person has, the lower their self-image.

How low is low?

The ultimate example of low self-esteem is Ex the Master Extractor. The Invisible Villain suffers from all twenty-eight forms of the *Emotional Virus*. Ex represents low self-esteem in its lowest of lowest forms.

This concludes the review of low self-esteem personalities.

What about these characters? Why do they act so terrible? How did they learn such dysfunctional behavior? Do they realize how bad they behave? Will they ever change?

After evaluating the list of low self-esteem personalities, a common response is, "Their personality traits are identical to many of the people I know or meet!" In reality, the vivid descriptions of the low self-esteem personalities are a rude awakening for all of us. The truth is, most people you come in contact with, everyone from perfect strangers to your closest loved ones, suffer from one or more forms of low self-esteem.

Most people you know suffer from multiple forms of the *Emotional Virus—The Dark Essence.*

The one person you fail to recognize as being infected with low self-image, the one person you most often overlook is, of course, yourself. As you ponder the behavior of low self-esteem characters, two questions must be answered. First, "How do low self-esteem people acquire such bad behavior in the first place?"

Second, "Why do people continue to practice, on a day to day basis, such emotionally crippling behavior?"

The answer is shockingly simple.

LEGACY OF BAD BEHAVIOR

The *Emotional Virus*—bad behavior—has been **unintentionally** passed from generation to generation since the beginning of recorded history. The *Emotional Virus* continues to spread undetected as normal, acceptable behavior as follows:

- **From parents and stepparents to the child.**
- **From grandparents to the child.**
- **From brothers/sisters/relatives to the child.**
- **From teachers/role models to the child.**
- **From the peer group to the child.**
- **From the media—television, movies, books, Internet, radio, video games, and music.**

IT IS NOT THEIR FAULT

It is important to remember that bad behavior is **unintentionally** passed to the next generation. No parent or teacher plots and plans to give low self-esteem to their children or students. They are <u>unaware</u> they are doing it; therefore, it is not their fault.

Throughout their entire adulthood, dysfunctional low self-esteem sufferers unknowingly teach bad behavior to their own children, spouse, friends, business associates, and social contacts without ever realizing it. In effect, by accident. Most people believe they are doing the right thing; after all, this is how they were raised by their parents and teachers. Because people with low self-esteem are raised in a dysfunctional family atmosphere, the chances of them passing low self-esteem behavioral traits on to their children is almost guaranteed.

Logically, you can trace your own genealogy of low self-esteem by simply reviewing your own family tree. "I got low self-esteem from my parents...who got it from their parents...who got it from their parents...and so on...and so on."

Each generation of parents faithfully passes on what they consider to be normal behavior to the next generation. This self-destructive cycle has been reoccurring for centuries, resulting in a world overrun with social, political, and economic turmoil.

AM I IN DENIAL

The fact is, low self-image promotes self-denial. Self-denial, or being "in denial", prevents you from making correct decisions and stands in the way of clear thinking. When you are in denial, you create a fake reality, destroying any chance you have to improve emotionally. Denial takes away your desire to change, robbing you of the highest truth. When you are in denial you experience emotional instability, and you refuse to admit it.

It is easier to tell yourself, "There is no problem," than to deal with the issues at hand. You hope the problem will go away by itself—disappear. Unfortunately, it never does.

Self-denial is learned. You are not born with it. Denial, like all other forms of the *Emotional Virus*, is acquired during childhood by observing your parents, siblings, relatives, and teachers—all of *them* living in denial.

AN EPIPHANY

You have now identified some low self-esteem characters and how they behave. Most likely you have experienced an epiphany, that "ahhha" moment when a "light bulb" illuminates in your mind and you suddenly realize a higher truth—a revelation. Your epiphany fills you with positive energy, a commitment to improve your behavior and a desire to change.

You have now put low self-esteem in proper perspective by identifying it. By recognizing the *Emotional Virus—The Dark Essence*—you have forced the sinister low self-esteem invaders from the dark shadows of human emotion into the bright sunlight of self-awareness. You are now aware of bad behavior and vow to eliminate it from your life. Your senses are magnified—keenly alert. You now see your friends and family in a different light. You are attentive, but cautious, as you observe low self-esteem behavior in action, "played out" before your very eyes.

You now realize how bad, dysfunctional behavior is acquired during childhood. You have found the first great treasure—Awareness. Self-awareness!

It is time to continue your journey, your search for Self—to discover who you are—so you may eliminate your own low self-image.

Your second Way To Change—Recognize High Self-Esteem—awaits you.

"There is no way to happiness;
happiness IS the way."

Chapter 2
Recognize High Self-Esteem

Self-esteem is a paradoxical term. The dictionary defines self-esteem as: *1. belief in oneself 2. undue pride in oneself.* Undue pride meaning conceited, narcissistic and vain. The two definitions are totally opposite, the first part describing high self-esteem and the second part describing low self-esteem.

To begin your second change—recognize high self-esteem—you must realize that:

Your Self-Esteem Is:
Who You Are
Your Individuality
Your Human Dignity
Your Unique Personality
Your External Life Force
Your Positive Energy Source

Your esteem is your perception of your Self, how you see your Self, what you think of your Self. How you feel about your Self is your most important reality.

You have either a positive image of your Self, defined as high self-esteem or, you have a negative image of your self, defined as low self-esteem.

When you have high self-esteem, you experience high vibrations of positive energy producing the highest thoughts. When you have low self-esteem, you experience low vibrations of negative energy producing the lowest thoughts.

Self-esteem is based on Law of Attraction: Like attracts like. Low self-esteem thoughts attract low energy responses from the universe. High self-esteem thoughts attract high energy responses from the universe.

QUEST FOR HIGH ESTEEM

Humans are esteem seekers constantly searching for ways to satisfy and replenish their fragile egos, their esteem. Your quest for esteem does not occur once a year, once a month, or once a day, but every waking moment.

The gratification of self-esteem is directly responsible for your emotional health. Until you satisfy your esteem's needs—until you quench your self-esteem's *thirst*—you are unable to take your mind off yourself, stop thinking of yourself and begin to think and care about your Self and therefore, others.

When your self-esteem is unsatisfied you are not on good terms with yourself; consequently, you are not on good terms with others. You do not have to look far in your search for a higher self-esteem. The people you love, the people you live and work with, hold the key to your self-esteem quest.

All you have to do is learn to like others by liking yourself, your Self. Maintaining a healthy esteem gives you the emotional tools to lead a functional and happy lifestyle.

The health of your esteem determines who you are.

A SLEEPLESS SELF-ESTEEM

To further understand your emotional needs, compare your self-esteem to a vital physical need—take sleep for instance. When you get enough rest each night you never think of sleep. But if you go too long without sleep your personality is guaranteed to change. Without sleep, you go from good natured and happy to angry, critical and despondent. You lash out at people if they so much as look at you funny. You cannot seem to get along with anyone—all you think about is sleep.

It will never help for someone to tell you, "Get your mind

off sleep!" "Quit thinking of yourself!" or "Stop worrying about your problems!", because your basic physical needs always come first. The only way to feel better is to get some sleep. The same with your self-esteem, it must be nurtured and properly cared for or you suffer emotionally.

NURTURE YOUR ESTEEM

Only when your essential physical needs are satisfied can you feel good about yourself. In comparison, only when your essential **emotional** needs are satisfied can you feel good about yourself. Only when you take good care of your own esteem will you experience true happiness and success.

Low self-esteem people lack a healthy esteem because they do not know how to take care of their emotional needs. Because they suffer from the *Emotional Virus*, they fail to take care of themselves, living a dysfunctional lifestyle.

HEALTHY ESTEEM

The secret to happiness is getting along with people, from family to total strangers. People with an unhealthy self-esteem are not emotionally equipped to interact with the people around them. Their daily routines are filled with self-created stress and turmoil. Their lives are empty and unfulfilled. Relationships fail, careers falter, health deteriorates—physically and emotionally.

People suffering from the *Emotional Virus* spend each day in behavioral chaos, a constant state of flux—a nightmare of negative thoughts. Unhealthy personalities experience negative, unhappy thoughts: "Is this all there is to life?" "I'm rich; why am I so miserable?" "I've got to gain control of my life!" "I have no friends!"

Sound familiar? It is the haunting voice of unhappiness, a mind filled with negative thoughts.

You finally admit, "Okay, I know my self-esteem's not as healthy as it could be. Deep down, I'm not happy." Then, you ask yourself, "How can I change?"

The answer is simple. Adopt the Esteem Creed.

THE ESTEEM CREED
- I constantly seek a healthy esteem to feel good about myself.
- I must take good care of my esteem.
- When I take care of my esteem I am on good terms with myself.
- When I am on good terms with myself I am on good terms with others.
- When I am on good terms with others I experience a higher self-esteem.
- High self-esteem guarantees happiness.

As you begin believing and living the Esteem Creed, you begin to trust yourself, to trust your thoughts, to trust other people. You recognize exactly what self-esteem looks like.

People with healthy self-esteem stand out from the crowd. They have energized auras. They possess magnetic personalities. They have a warm glow about them. People with healthy self-esteems possess recognizable personality traits.

High self-esteem people are: *Ambitious, Admired, Brave, Confident, Charismatic, Cheerful, Carefree, Courageous, Conversationalists, Determined, Devoted, Dedicated, Delightful, Ethical, Enthusiastic, Eager, Exceptional, Exciting, Energetic, Entrancing, Enlightened, Friendly, Functional, Faithful, Fun To Be With, Fair, Free, Honest, Happy, Honorable, Impartial, Ingenious, Inspirational, Intelligent, Loyal, Loving, Listeners, Leaders, Moral, Noble, Optimistic, Prosperous, Patient, Passionate, Powerful, Proud, Peaceful, Positive, Relaxed, Remarkable, Respectable, Successful, Sensitive, Self-Motivating, Spirited, Sensible, Sincere, Safe, Sympathetic, Trustworthy, Truthful, Untroubled, Unbiased, Understanding, Unforgettable, Vivacious, Warm, Wonderful, and Utopian.*

YOUR BIRTHRIGHT IS HAPPINESS

Happy individuals who experience positive thoughts do exist. At first, these high self-esteem people might seem few and far between or hard to find. But now that you have experienced your first two changes, you begin to recognize people with positive energy, with healthy egos. Once you become enlightened, you notice more of them than you ever imagined.

As you uncover the secret to a higher self-esteem, you find yourself attracted to these positive energy people. You feel yourself wanting to be near them. You have committed to making them part of your life.

You can spot them in a crowd, sense their presence when they share the same room with you. When these high self-esteem people speak to you or shake your hand, you instantly sense their undeniable warmth and charisma—their aura—positive energy. You want to know them, talk to them. You desire to be just like them.

ESTEEM—HIGH OR LOW?

Now that you have reviewed the first and second changes comparing low self-esteem and high self-esteem personality traits, the first question you must answer is: "Do I, myself, have low self-esteem or high self-esteem?"

Well, there is good news, and bad news. The good news is, you, and most of the people you know or meet, possess one or more high self-esteem personality traits.

The bad news is: for each high self-esteem trait, you, and most of the people you know or meet, have **twice as many** low self-esteem traits—bad behavior that dominates their lives.

Since you live in a society dominated by low self-esteem behavior (unknowingly, of course), most people suffer from dysfunctional, bad habits. High self-esteem behavior seems to shine through only on rare occasions. Clearly, your commitment to change must begin by eliminating all symptoms of low self-esteem behavior from your life. Now, not later.

YOUR LIFE SCRIPT

Your **physical** life story, your life script, begins at birth and ends at death. Like a wonderful play or movie, your life script has a first half, an intermission, and a second half—the conclusion and ending. The first part of your life script, the first few scenes, are written for you by your parents, peer group, teachers and television, movies, Internet—the media.

As you enter puberty, the plot thickens. By your teens you should be writing your own life script; yet, all too often your life script has already been written for you by the same people who wrote the opening scenes.

But you must not be discouraged. Like all great plays and unforgettable movies, it is intermission time. For you, it means time for rewrites and revisions—for making changes—for creating a happy ending.

If you find the first part of your life story to be unacceptable, if the beginning of your life script is not what you had hoped for, you now have the opportunity to write a remarkable second half, a blazing finish, an award-winning ending.

You may redeem the unacceptable first part of your life script right this moment. You simply need to agree you have reached *life's intermission* and the best is yet to come—the happy ending.

In concluding your second way to change, your epiphany has put high self-esteem in proper perspective.

At last, you realize exactly what high self-esteem people act like. You want to be just like them.

You now understand esteem and how it relates to a happy and functional lifestyle. You have discovered that a purposeful life, a life full of passion, exists by discovering who you truly are. You have discovered your self. Self.

By recognizing high self-esteem, you have obtained the second great treasure—health. Emotional health, as well a physical health, will soon be yours to embrace.

You may proceed to the third Way To Change and Discover Others—Discover Self.

Chapter 3
Discover Others – Discover Self

You will now learn to deal with people so your self-esteem and their self-esteem remain emotionally healthy. As you prepare for your third change, your goal is to maintain the self-esteem—the spirit and individuality—of everyone you come in contact with. This means your parents, your spouse, your children, your in-laws, your coworkers, your boss, business and social contacts, perfect strangers—everyone.

You will soon uncover valuable clues revealing answers to the questions: "How do I get along with people—find romance—make new friends—maintain a functional relationship with the one I love?"

Your self-success with relationships depends on your sincerity and recognition.

SINCERITY

You must believe people are important—sincerely believe it. Being real is your most important asset. Real means being honest, truthful, ethical, high-minded and trustworthy. Sincerity sets the stage for success. People sense your sincerity, your realness. You cannot fake your true feelings.

The truth is: every individual is a treasure of untold knowledge and adventure just waiting to be enjoyed. Every person has a wonderful story to tell. If you are unwilling to believe people are important, sincerely believe it, you are doomed to a lifetime of frustration, failure and unhappiness.

The best way to show others you care is to acknowledge their presence, give them your undivided attention.

Recognition makes people feel wanted, feel appreciated, feel important. Recognition of others reveals your sincerity.

RECOGNITION

If you are totally honest with yourself you will admit you want something from other people. In other words, sales people want your business, politicians want your vote, teachers want your undivided attention. Your employer wants your cooperation, production and loyalty. Your family wants your love, attention and guidance. Your friends want your friendship.

So admit it, you *do* want things from the people around you and there is one thing you desire more than any other—the one gratifying, esteem-boosting, emotional prize you crave the most—recognition.

So, how do you go about obtaining the one prize you desire most? Easy. The only way to successfully get what you want—recognition—is to give the people around you what they want first. How do you do that? By paying attention to others—discovering others!

You will never discover others, one of the greatest assets in your quest for self-success, until you learn to pay attention.

LACK OF ATTENTION

As you have just learned, paying attention to the people around us, giving them your undivided attention and recognizing their uniqueness, is one of the keys to your success at home, at work, and everywhere you go.

Failure to recognize the people around you, known as lack of attention, lack of training and lack of leadership, creates children and adults who will do anything, who will stop at nothing, for attention.

Lack of attention creates naughty children, undisciplined teenagers, unproductive employees, unfaithful spouses, and totally dysfunctional adults.

Some familiar examples are:

"Undisciplined Children"

The main reason children are naughty and do not mind their parents is lack of attention. Children crave recognition and emotional support from their parents, and when these young, impressionable members of society are ignored, the results are often disastrous.

You can easily spot a child lacking attention. They cry out, "Look at me!" "Watch this!" "Mommy, Daddy, pay attention!"

They are naughty for one reason, they expect their parents to pay attention to them. Children do not understand emotional neglect, social abandonment, or failure to communicate. Children must be acknowledged.

Keep in mind, parents fail to recognize their own children for one reason: as children their parents did not pay attention to them. As young adults they were subjected to parental comments such as, "Not now!" or "Can't you see I'm busy!" or "Stop nagging, we'll get together soon!"

Paying attention, specifically, spending valuable time together, was not priority to their parents. Understandably, it is not priority in raising their own children.

Lack of attention allows the low self-esteem disease to survive from one generation to the next.

"Misbehaving Teenagers"

The main reason teenagers misbehave is lack of attention. Children raised by inattentive parents eventually grow up to be large unmanageable children known as teenagers. These dysfunctional young adults are rebellious because they crave attention—they want to be noticed. With a dysfunctional adulthood looming in their future, only one thing can save these neglected teenagers—attention. Parents shake their heads and admit, "Ever since I started working she's been so rebellious!" "I try to spend more time with my kids, but I'm too busy!" "My folks both worked and look how good I turned out!" "I give my kids everything I didn't have as a child and they're still not happy!"

After shaking their heads in confusion, parents end with one final complaint, "I don't understand why my own kids have become so uncooperative and distant." "What is wrong with them?" "What is their problem?"

Proof of emotional neglect is in the air—it is everywhere. Just listen to teenagers complain, "My parents don't understand me or my problems." "Mom and Dad always ignore me!" or "I wonder if my folks even know I exist?" "I'm leaving home as soon as I'm old enough to get away from my parents."

If parents expect love and cooperation, their motto must be, it is never too late to begin paying attention.

"Unproductive Employees"

The main reason employees are unhappy and unproductive is lack of attention, appropriately known as lack of training.

Employees need to be trained and then told how they are doing. Workers, wanting to do a good job and seeking praise, constantly ask themselves, "Am I doing this correctly?" "What does my boss think of my work?" or mumble, "My supervisor never talks to me unless I'm doing something wrong!"

Negative attention is counter productive. Employees must train with positive attention, with positive criticism. The best way to show recognition towards workers is with proper training, followed with frequent reminders of how they are doing—reinforcing their self-esteem, their fragile egos.

"Criminal Activity"

The main reason for the majority of crimes and unnecessary acts of violence is lack of attention. Stemming from a low self-esteem childhood, the dysfunctional person is merely crying out, "Look at me!" "Pay attention!" "Help me!" When no one responds to their desperate cry for help, the despondent person robs the local liquor store, kidnaps someone, or murders innocent people—all for attention—recognition!

Survivors of dysfunctional childhoods rationalize, "This will show them!" "I'll prove I'm important!" "This will get my face on national television!" "They'll all be sorry they didn't listen to me!"

"Loneliness and Depression"

The main reason people suffer from loneliness and depression is lack of attention—self-attention. Loneliness, another word for lack of happiness or self-fulfillment, is given to you in childhood by unknowingly neglectful parents, and dwells in your thoughts during adulthood.

Most lonely people live with another person or their family. They are not physically alone, but emotionally alone. They create your own self-imposed loneliness just for attention.

The cure for loneliness? Improve your self-image. As your self-esteem increases your loneliness decreases.

When you discover **who you are** on your journey of esteem, you begin feeling good about yourself as you acquire a healthy self-image. Your loneliness and depression disappear. You feel worthwhile—special.

YOU ARE BORN PERFECT

You are born perfect—special—as a unique individual. If you are not raised special, told and shown you are special, you lose your special feeling—your self-worth and self-respect. Special don't mean getting ribbons and trophies, or feeling entitled.

When you are told by parents and teachers, "You won't amount to anything", your chances of future success and happiness are greatly diminished.

When you are told by childhood guardians, "You are worthless", you grow up feeling worthless. When you are made to feel guilty or ashamed of yourself as young adults, you carry those low self-image curses with you the rest of your life—a hopeless feeling.

Remember your life script? You agreed you cannot change the first part of your life story, but you *do* have total control over the outcome.

Your life is about to change. Once you believe you are special, you become special. You have so much to offer yourself, the people in your life, and society. No matter what you heard as a child, no matter what you are told as an adult, from this day forward, no one can take away your dignity.

You now begin to recognize who you are, why you are here, where you are going. You have the power to make everyone you touch feel special, truly special.

In concluding your third great change, you now realize every human being needs recognition—to be discovered. When someone notices you, it is always a huge compliment.

Because they are recognizing your importance, your uniqueness and individuality, your goal must be to make other people feel important too.

If you expect to become a successful business person, a popular manager, a wonderful parent and a dynamic leader, you must discover the secret to success in business, parenting, and social life, you must learn to deal with people—discover others.

By discovering others you now feel comfortable with yourself—your Self. You now see the important role people play in your continual quest for a higher self-image, and that self-respect is earned by getting along with others.

Wealth, the third great treasure, is now yours. Wealth means a poverty of desires. Wealth means needing nothing, enjoying all things.

Continue your inner journey on the Great Way—the Open Road, with the fourth Way To Change: Silence—Learn To Listen.

*"Those who know do not talk;
those who talk do not know."*

Chapter 4
Silence — Learn To Listen

During the previous three Way To Changes, you identified bad behavior from good behavior, inspiring you to discover who you are. You identified low self-esteem personalities, how to recognize high self-esteem, and that the elimination of low self-image begins by discovering others and then, discovering your Self.

With the fourth Way To Change, and all remaining changes, you implement positive actions allowing you to:
- Listen Attentively
- Think Positive Thoughts
- Act with Confidence
- Overcome Fears
- Eliminate Stress
- Conquer Bad Habits
- Get Along with Others
- Control Anger
- Change Your Thoughts
- Praise Properly
- Criticize Correctly
- Provide Leadership

Now that you have identified low self-esteem personalities, you immediately notice one glaring character trait they all have in common: people with low self-esteem seldom listen and never stop talking—they will not be quiet. They are *Talkaholics*.

What causes this unacceptable and annoying behavior?

The answer is, when a person's self-esteem, or ego, is unhealthy, all they think about is themselves and their own problems—they are unable to turn their attention to others. Sound familiar? Even though you love your parents, your spouse, your children, and your friends, you often do not allow them to get a word in edgewise. You fail to listen. You unintentionally shut others out. You often out-talk everyone around you.

The fourth part of your journey toward change teaches you yet another way to eliminate low self-esteem behavior from your daily life: simply begin listening to others.

By sincerely listening to the person talking and not thinking about yourself, or interrupting, you immediately experience a higher self-image. When you listen, you recognize the other person's importance and you become their trusted friend.

Understanding your own self-esteem only happens by first understanding others. How are you going to understand others if you never listen?

Before the discussion of self-esteem listening skills, remember one important fact: every person has one favorite subject—**themselves.**

When you acknowledge the other person's favorite subject (themselves) by listening to their every word, only *then* will you understand your own Self and how to acquire a healthy self-image.

LISTENING SKILLS

Not talking about yourself, better known as the art of listening, is an extremely challenging life-style change. After all, you grew up emulating your parents and teachers who often lacked good listening skills. As children, how many times were you told, "Children should be seen and not heard." or "Do not speak until you're spoken to." or "Be quiet!" or "Go away, I'm busy now."

More often than not, you were never asked to speak because your parents seemed to talk until they were blue in the face. They did not seem to have the time or the interest to listen to what you had to say. As a result, you immediately mastered pro-talk and anti-listening skills, with interrupting and raising your voice as your main *weapons* to compete with family, relatives, and friends.

You have unknowingly become a professional interrupter and loudmouth conversationalist specializing in ignoring, out-talking, and verbally overpowering everyone around you. Why? Because you grew up a poor listener.

Being able to focus and concentrate on another person's conversation is a lost and dying attribute of human society, one that must be re-learned, or in most cases, learned from scratch. You must continually remind yourself: nothing is more interesting than the other person—nothing.

Below are five esteem listening skills that help you provide leadership to the people you live with, work with, and play with.

1. Pay Attention

Every human being has a wonderful story to tell. When you sincerely begin to like and appreciate others, you begin listening to what they have to say.

As you learn to listen you must deeply concentrate on what people are saying—pay total attention.

People immediately know if you are paying attention to what they are saying; they sense your disinterest.

Look them straight in the eyes while they speak.

2. Show Interest

Folding your arms, looking around, sighing, yawning, or rolling your eyes shows lack of interest. It is important to make eye contact with the person talking—it is your signal to the speaker that you are truly listening.

Sincerely respond to the speaker's story by leaning forward and nodding your head as if to respond, "Yes, I understand!" "I get what you're saying!" Listening and maintaining sincere interest might be difficult at first; after all, you are often the one *doing* all the talking.

3. Ask For More

Learning to ask questions without distracting the person talking. Make sure you wait for the end of the explanation or story before you ask a question. Appropriate timing, patience, is critical to your success and happiness. Sometimes by waiting patiently, you might forget what you were going to ask, but as long as you allow the other person to continue speaking, you have accomplished your goal.

If you truly appreciate what is being said, interjecting phrases such as, "Go on!" "Tell me more!" "How exciting!" or simply smiling or nodding, lets the person know you are listening. You must, of course, *be* sincerely listening or your self-centered personality will rear its ugly head and you will interrupt or show disinterest.

4. Never Interrupt

Always allow the person talking to finish his or her story. Never interrupt or cut them off short. If a real emergency or critical issue suddenly arises, let the other person know you look forward to continuing the conversation as soon as possible, reminding them you value what they have to say.

When your cell phone rings and they say, "Go ahead, get that call", always respond, "No, talking to you is more important!"

It is so easy to allow daily distractions to interfere with your attention span and disrupt your listening skills. Disruptive behavior leaves a negative impression on the people you ignore, interrupt, place on call-waiting, or brush-off. You might as well announce, "You're not as important as this phone call!"

5. Compliment Others

An excellent way to make the speaker feel important is by repeating their words or phrases. For example, when someone tells you, "I'm from New York," by simply repeating, "New York! Great city!" you let them know you enjoy their company.

You are literally telling them, "Yes, I am listening; you are important." Seemingly stupid, silly, or trite comments such as, "Really!" "You don't say!" "That's wonderful!" or "How exciting!" are direct indicators you appreciate the speaker's story. The other person feels recognized.

Adding simple one-liners such as "Right!" or "I understand!" are excellent ways to introduce your own ideas or suggestions without opposition. The speaker knows that to disagree with your ideas is the same as putting down their *own* ideas.

Complimenting other people, whether it is your child, your spouse, your boss, or someone you have just met, is accomplished by adding short, attentive responses while you are truly listening, looking them in the eyes.

The five self-esteem listening skills work. Use them daily.

THE UNACCEPTABLES

Learning to listen also means becoming aware of the complex world around us. As you sharpen your listening skills your other self-esteem senses improve, not just the way your eyes view the world and the people in it, but more importantly, how your sixth sense—your intuition—your own esteem—perceives the complexities of human nature.

As your self-esteem senses become fine-tuned you are able to identify symptoms of the *Emotional Virus*—emotional diseases—affecting everyone around you. Typical behavior accepted by people as perfectly normal but identifiable as low self-esteem behaviors, are known as the *Unacceptables*. Unacceptable behavior occurs billions of times each day. Can you name some *Unacceptables*? Here are a few to contemplate.

UNACCEPTABLES

Anger, temper fits, domestic violence (such as spanking a child, hitting a spouse, striking a stranger or kicking a dog), revenge, emotional harm to others, screaming at a child, screaming at a spouse, screaming at employees, screaming at other drivers, harassing strangers, picking a fight, judging people before you meet them, judging people after you meet them, hating others, impatience, sighing, tapping your fingers, mean looks, threatening stares, staying in bed all day and blaming depression, overeating and blaming depression, sulking, abusing food, greed, stealing, selfishness, gossiping about family, friends and relatives, spreading rumors, gossiping about coworkers.

Telling racist jokes, laughing at sexist jokes, enjoying ethnic jokes, sexism, lust, sexual harassment, envy, feeling jealous, throwing jealous rages, bragging about past exploits, criticizing your competition, outdoing friends and relatives, outshining guests, interrupting, talking out of turn, beating children at games, feeling guilty, feeling insecure, telling secrets, ignoring praise and talking too much.

Inability to finish projects, feeling ashamed, not allowing events to happen naturally, living beyond your means, making excuses, begging for love, begging for forgiveness, allowing people's behavior to affect you, believing you know what is best for others, provoking others, lacking self-control, ignoring problems, making people mad, instigating arguments, worrying sick over loved ones, abusing drugs, drinking excessive alcoholic beverages, afraid to make mistakes, taking things personally, believing you are not good enough, fearing rejection.

Being controlled by events, allowing others to control you, not taking yourself seriously, expecting perfection, feeling suicidal, believing you are helpless victims, embarrassing easily, always apologizing, being in denial, saying one thing and meaning another, fear of failure, fear of success, fear of aging, fear of death, losing sleep over problems, allowing others to hurt you physically and emotionally.

MORE UNACCEPTABLES

Extramarital affairs, sexual abuse, acting irresponsibly, failing to eat sensibly, failing to exercise, seducing others, abusive language, demanding ultimatums, not feeling approval from your parents, remaining in dysfunctional relationships, bribing others, not budgeting finances, unplanned parenthood, sticking your nose where it does not belong, hating how you look, blaming your parents, telling others what you think they want to hear, catching people doing something wrong, being lazy, not trusting your feelings or decisions, not trusting other people, rejecting compliments.

Always crying, whining, non-stop nagging, lying to others, lying to yourself, cheating on taxes, falsifying your resume, feeling stupid, giving up without trying, expecting someone else to make you happy, really believing you cannot live without someone, and lastly—failing to love yourself, and therefore, others.

SURVIVORS OF LOW SELF-ESTEEM CHILDHOODS

Who are the survivors of low self-esteem childhoods? They are your friends, the people at work, your relatives, and your immediate family members. You might ask, "Am I?"

The secret to self-happiness, the way to eliminate sadness and depression, is to know where you came from. Admit how you were raised and evaluate your childhood with a kind heart, a gentle spirit and an open mind.

You know the truth. Most likely, you are a survivor. You, your friends and relatives, are survivors of low self-esteem childhoods—victims of unacceptable behavior. You received little or no recognition as a child, were ignored, or even worse, beaten, abused and told you would not amount to anything.

No one planned your fate. Your parents and teachers were simply victims of the same treatment themselves. They too were victims of unacceptable behavior—survivors of low self-esteem childhoods.

Your childhood is over. You are no longer a victim. Being a victim is part of your past. You are now in charge of your life, in control of your fate. You have heard all the childhood horror stories. It is time to stop the stories and begin healing yourself. Embrace the power of silence.

THE POWER OF SILENCE

Silence allows freedom within—an internal quietness that allows an inner reality. Silence allows peaceful thoughts and relaxation. This can only happen through meditation.

Simply sit in a quiet place and allow your thoughts to slow down. Hear yourself breathe. Close your eyes and feel the bliss.

Talk to your soul while you meditate. Your soul is your divine spark, your Self. Your soul is keenly aware of things your mind can barely conceive. Your soul, your quintessence, is not a thing inside you, it is all of you, all around you. Your soul is unique from what you think of as yourself—your Self.

All souls in the universe form one, infinite mass of energy. This means humans are all one, both physically and metaphysically. The soul is not a physical, tangible thing. Although you picture your soul as this entity, this *thing* inside you, the soul cannot be touched. Your soul resides in the world of invisibility.

Just like magnetism exists in the invisible world—the imaginal world—so does your soul exist. The imaginal world is real. When you feel it, embrace it. Then, you will feel your soul.

It is important to talk to your soul because your soul always tells the truth. Your soul does not spend time thinking, it acts instantly. Your soul knows what is best for you. You never get in trouble listening to your soul. Your soul voice is not one of language—inner dialogue, but the voice of intuition—spirituality.

The soul speaks through your heart and ignores logic. The soul speaks no words, simply vibrations. You can feel when the soul guides you; it is totally different from when your mind tells you what to do.

Once you experience internal peace and quiet—silence, you will perceive your world as more meaningful and get in touch with your soulfulness—your soul voice.

Learn to listen. Learn to sit still and be quiet. Learn silence, quiet your mind. Then, and only then, will you hear your soul voice. It is the voice of universal love and compassion, the voice that is heard throughout the cosmos. The soul voice speaks during your most troubling times and during your most celebrated moments. The soul speaks to you in dreams and during meditation. When the soul voice speaks, you feel a sense of goodness inside. Sometimes your soul voice comforts you during your most sorrowful times, your deepest agonies. Your soul voice has only your best interest in mind. Just listen and you will hear heavenly music until the end of time, forever.

THE HIGHEST CHOICE

Your quest to change your thoughts begins by asking questions. Admit that the only thing you truly know is that you know nothing.

Never accept the word or teachings of others. This includes the words in this book. Continue to seek wisdom so you may decide for yourself. Make up your own mind. Do not allow others to think for you.

Ask yourself, "Does the information in this book reveal the highest truth?"

When you know the wisdom to be true, ask yourself the ultimate question. "Whenever I have to make a decision, what choice puts me on the high road?" The high road is the path of truth—the highest choice. Also known as The Great Way.

Each time you have to make a choice, you stand at the crossroads of decision. One direction takes you down the low road; the opposite direction takes you up the high road.

During your childhood, you were taken down the low road, the path of deceit, the road to ruin. Most likely, you have traveled the low road most of your life.

The low road is the road to confusion, the path to greed, profit and exploitation, the road to self-indulgence, the road most people follow.

The high road is the path of honesty, the highest truth. You might know this path as *the road less traveled.*

When you fail to find the high road it is because you live in a low self-esteem fog and cannot see the path before you.

So, you choose the low road. When you stand at the crossroads of decision and face a choice of which road to travel, you avoid the high road paved with truth because you believe the low road is easier, less work, less pain. But eventually, the low road, full of ruts, always ends in anxiety, fear, and failure.

The ultimate question is, "What is the highest choice I can make right now, this moment in time?" If answered truthfully, this most basic of questions will change your life immediately.

The truth will set you free.

Choosing the highest truth is the ultimate freedom-within experience. Make the highest choice; you will never take the low road again. You will never be lost.

In concluding your fourth Way To Change, listening takes on new meaning, especially silence. You have the right to be happy, and now that you have found the high road, the path to happiness and self-fulfillment, nothing can stop you.

Nothing or no thing.

With this new epiphany you have discovered that believing in the importance of others and what others have to say; then, listening to your self, awards you with the fourth great treasure—Honesty.

Your new awareness allows you to begin the fifth Way To Change: Never Say "I" Until Asked.

"You get what you think about, whether you want it or not."

Chapter 5
Never Say "I" Until Asked

You are about to discover why the word "I" is so critical to your future success and happiness. You have learned that your most important, knowledgeable, and favorite conversational subject is your self. "Me, myself, and I" is your best and most exciting subject, and there is nothing wrong with that. After all, you are an expert on yourself and your own unique life experiences. You can talk about yourself all day and all night long. You are capable of non-stop talk.

THE ULTIMATE TRUTH

When you have a healthy self-esteem, a content ego, you no longer have to talk about yourself. You know exactly who you are, you are comfortable with yourself. High self-esteem gives you total peace of mind.

When you continually talk about yourself you do <u>not</u> have a healthy esteem, you suffer from low self-image. You do not have a clue who you are—you feel terribly alone—you are always depressed—happiness is short-lived—your life is in chaos.

The only way to improve your life and gain self-esteem, begin to feel good about yourself, figure out who you really are, is to stop talking about yourself and start listening to others.

You will realize the less you say "I" (talk about yourself) the higher your self-esteem rises. By eliminating "I", you become a better person. By listening, you discover who you are.

Beginning today, your will deal with people by not saying "I" during conversations.

It will take tremendous concentration, personal stamina, and commitment. Beads of sweat will form on your forehead—your idle tongue will twitch—your eyes will water—your lips will quiver—your brain will blow all fuses, but you must not, under any circumstances, say "I".

By now you must be muttering to yourself, "Do I have to go the rest of *my* life without talking about *my* all-time favorite subject—ME?"

The answer is, "Of course not! You will have plenty of opportunities to talk about your favorite subject, yourself."

For example:

You May Say "I" When:

- Another person asks you a question.
- You are complimenting or thanking someone.
- You are relating to another person's story.
- You are invited as a guest speaker.
- You are asked to give a presentation.

NEVER SAY "I KNOW"

Quite often during conversations, you matter-of-factly blurt out, "I know!" while the other person is talking. Three reasons you consciously or unconsciously interject the phrase "I know" is to: (a) let the other person know you are intelligent, or, (b) perhaps you are already aware of the answer to the problem, or (c) you are insulted the subject was brought up in the first place.

Admittedly, if you really listen to the popular interjection "I know!" it often comes off as defensive, spiteful or oversensitive.

Even if you do know what is being explained, it is always best to remain silent and not attempt to prove you already know what the speaker knows, or let them know you are just as smart.

By remaining silent, you allow the speaker the glory of the moment. They respect you more for your attentive listening, not for your defensive-sounding, interruptive, "I Know!"

HIGH SELF-ESTEEM TALK

Happiness and self-confidence depend on your ability to communicate and talk effectively: to express your ideas, desires, ambitions, goals, fears and disappointments with emotional honesty. Talk is critical for maintaining a healthy self-esteem.

Talk is important, not vocabulary. You do not have to be a living dictionary, walking encyclopedia, or literary genius. The most important thing to remember is, when you are asked to talk, you make the most of the opportunity, not by blurting out "I" or "I know" every other word, but by carefully listening and waiting for the correct moment to reply.

The best way to master high self-esteem talk is to build a bridge of words between yourself and the person, or persons, you are talking to. A bridge of words opens up communication lines between yourself and the rest of society.

BUILDING A BRIDGE OF WORDS

The five steps to build your bridge of words are:

1. **Begin Talking With Casual Conversation**
2. **Get People Talking About Themselves**
3. **Agree Most Of The Time**
4. **Form A Human Relations Bond**
5. **Never Outshine The Other Person**

1. Begin Talking With Casual Conversation

Casual conversation works with total strangers as well as with people you have known all your life. Casual conversation is, "What a great day!" or "Where did you get those shoes?" or "I hear you just bought a new computer!" These seemingly simple statements get the conversation going so you can get into deeper conversation. It creates a comfort zone.

The first rule is, do not try too hard, just relax. You must be yourself as you start the conversation. Worrying about sounding stupid, boring, unintelligent or silly is your worst enemy. Trying to sound brilliant may immediately "turn off" the other person.

Warm up slowly—go easy. By being sincere and positive, other people open up like books, strangers feel they have known you for years—they become comfortable around you.

2. Get People Talking About Themselves

Always ask questions concerning the other person's favorite subject, the one thing they are an absolute expert on—**themselves.** If you really think about it, people never run out of self-information; that is, stories about themselves.

Your success depends on your ability to focus and concentrate on the other person's story and not think of yourself—to remain silent.

Why? Since most people you talk to suffer from low self-esteem, you seldom get the chance to mention what a wonderful person *you* are because they seldom ask. You are lucky to get a word in edgewise.

Your job is to *bite your tongue* and listen. The reward for such heroism? A higher self-image! Remember, you will always feel better about yourself at the end of any conversation when you realize you did not *need* to talk about yourself.

3. Agree Most Of The Time

Maintain the other person's self-esteem and ego at all costs. Even when they give the wrong score to the ball game, or mispronounce a word, or make an incorrect statement—let it go.

Ask yourself, "Will it really make any difference if I correct and possibly embarrass them, or am I putting them in their place to make myself look and feel superior?"

The only time to politely but firmly disagree is when the statement could lead to physical harm such as, "The gun's not loaded!" "Smoking cigarettes is good for you!" or possible emotional stress such as, "Your income taxes aren't due until July 15th!"

When you feel it is absolutely necessary to correct another person, positive criticism is the most effective way to deal with the other person and maintain their self-respect, especially their respect for you. Your ability to agree with others lets them know you are on their side. You establish you are not out to get them, you are not the enemy, you are on their team.

4. Form A Human Relations Bond

There are specific times during a conversation when you may say "I" or briefly mention yourself when the statement ties in or directly relates to the speaker's subject.

For example, when someone exclaims, "Our family always vacationed at Yosemite," you may add, "Really? So did our family!"

By relating to the other person's story, it allows you the opportunity to tell the person a little about yourself, and more importantly, it forms a human relations bond.

A human relations bond enables others to feel important because you share their same interests, goals, or backgrounds. Anything that makes you "be like" the other person helps them to immediately like you.

Keep your statement brief, a few words. Never use conversation as a launching pad for a rude interruption.

5. Never Outshine The Other Person

Because you constantly seek praise and recognition you are always anxious to impress others with your own importance. You might think, "I can't wait to impress them with my knowledge!" or "I'll blow them away with my wonderful personality!" "I'll knock 'em dead!" or "They're really going to love this story!"

However, based on everything you have learned thus far, the only way to effectively impress the other person is to let them know you are impressed by them.

The secret to your success is your ability to get the other person talking about their all-time favorite subject—**themselves**. Whether you have just met the person for the first time, or have known the person for years, you must allow the other person center stage.

By making them the "star of the show", you experience personal growth beyond your wildest dreams, both emotionally and socially.

High self-esteem conversation makes a complete stranger feel like they have known you for years. More importantly, the people you have known for years feel they have met a brand new person. For indeed, they have!

What is truly amazing is that high self-esteem talk involves more listening than talking. What a concept!

IDENTIFY LOW SELF-ESTEEM CONVERSATIONS

Low self-esteem conversations occur every day of your life—at home, at school, at work, at play, and in personal relationships—everywhere you go.

Like all low self-esteem behaviors, you learn the "language of the lowly" as children and young adults.

It is just a matter of time before you become experts in the use of low self-esteem conversation—"shock talk"—by watching your peers, role models and media heroes.

Sad but true, the majority of media: Internet, television, radio, books, video games, music and movies reinforce negative communication techniques. Everywhere you turn you are exposed to dysfunctional discussions—low self-esteem conversations—unacceptable talk.

Examples of low self-esteem conversations are:

"The Interruption"

A friend tells you about a wonderful experience she has just had and before the words are barely out of her mouth, you interrupt with "I know!" as you begin describing a similar experience that has just happened to you. "I-I-I ... I-Me-My ... I-I-I," blares from your mouth as you completely forget what your friend just said. You might as well have announced, "I don't care about you or your story, *I am* more important...my story is much more exciting...be quiet and listen to me!"

"The Bragging Contest"

Your friends gather to chat socially. John, beaming with pride, begins the conversation by announcing the incredibly huge fish he caught over the weekend. With the words barely out of his mouth, he is rudely interrupted by Mary, bragging that "once upon a vacation" the fish she caught was much, much, much bigger.

No sooner does Mary begin telling her sensational story when Michael, loud and belligerently boisterous, brags, "I hold the world's record for the largest fish ever caught!"

You and the remaining group of frustrated and bewildered participants attempt to interrupt with your own experiences, while others walk away due to insults or disinterest.

The "let's outdo each other bragging contest" has frustrated everyone, but John and Mary pretend not to show it, while big-mouth Michael basks in his own glory, beaming with a false sense of being the most important.

"The Round Robin Put Down"

You are standing by the coffee machine at work, anxiously awaiting today's rumors, gossip and organizational tabloid-tidbits when Judy, a coworker, barely gets "good morning" out of her mouth when she begins gossiping about fellow employees.

It is normal to gossip about others, so you join in, and besides, it makes you feel good about yourself.

As the two of you "rip apart" the staff, Harold, your boss, approaches you and loudly criticizes your job performance in front of everyone and he abruptly marches away. Two more coworkers, Tom and Betty, rush to your aid.

Soon, the "low self-esteem chant" begins. Judy is making negative remarks about fellow workers, Tom is moaning and complaining about his paycheck, Betty is making fun of the boss behind his back, and you are putting down, bad-mouthing and making fun of everyone in the organization not in the room. It is a full-fledged "round robin put down".

"The Body Slam"

School has just let out. Your circle of close friends, your all-important peer group, gather in the hall. Your two best buddies, Ted and Bill, notice that Barry is wearing new boots. Ted points at the boots and sarcastically shouts, "Nice boots...for a wimp!"

While the entire group breaks into hysterical laughter and points, Bill adds, "Man, I wouldn't be caught dead in those things!" Barry, trying to be "cool" and remain part of the group, struggles to crack a smile.

But Barry is deeply hurt for he has received the ultimate put down by his friends—a vicious "body slam." In other words, the ego-crushing, low self-esteem put down has the same effect on Barry as picking him up and slamming him to the ground.

Stunned, Barry timidly lowers his head. Ted and Bill jeeringly exclaim, "Just kidding!" while the sardonic duo quickly scan the schoolyard for another victim to body slam.

With one sarcastic remark, Barry's self-image and fragile ego has been shattered, while the entire group has falsely elevated themselves—made themselves feel better at the expense of another individual—a friend.

MAGIC CIRCLE CONVERSATION

Now that you have discovered what high self-esteem talk and low self-esteem conversation sound like, it is time you discover the perfect form of human conversation between two or more persons—the magic circle conversation.

Since you have been exposed to non-functional conversation all your life, you must forget the past and open your mind. A magic circle conversation—functional conversation—between yourself and other people with healthy esteem sounds like this:

- You begin the functional conversation with a warm and friendly greeting.
- The other person immediately asks about you (your favorite subject).
- You finish discussing your topic and immediately turn your attention back to them (their favorite subject).
- They talk about themselves, or a personal experience, and immediately turn the spotlight back on you. Then, you get to talk about yourself, your favorite subject.
- And so on, and so on—a friendly, functional, give and take conversation.

Every magic circle conversation has high self-esteem dialogue, the dynamic exchange of functional communication. During a magic circle conversation you experience fair exchange—give and take—all parties win.

Everyone benefits. Everyone is happy.

There are no rude interruptions, no sudden interjections, no yawning or rolling of the eyes, only functional conversation. You maintain their self-esteem and they maintain your self-esteem.

How simple. This magic circle stuff is not so difficult, or is it?

When was the last time you overheard a magic circle conversation? Was it at home? How about at work? Maybe during school? Could it have been on television or at the movies, or in a book, or on the Internet?

You have to admit, you might *never* have initiated, been involved in, overheard, or witnessed a true fair-exchange of words—a magic circle conversation. Needless to say, when you attempt your first magic circle conversation, do not get too upset when the other person breaks the magic circle and fails to ask about you. Remember, that person does not know any better. They do not know what you know, for they have yet to experience their first epiphany of change.

Overlooking other peoples inability to carry on a functional discussion—magic circle conversation—becomes a daily experience for you. You must be patient.

The chances of finding someone capable of a magic circle conversation is rare when you first begin your journey. Your quest for esteem might be lonely at first, but things will change because you will begin to seek out people with positive energy.

In concluding your fifth Way To Change, you discover that less is better. Less talk and more listening results in more friends, sound relationships, a better marriage, a more productive career—a happy lifestyle.

You realize that talking about yourself, especially your overuse and abuse of the ever-popular "I" word, is the last thing other people want to hear (low self-esteem people, that is). Less talk becomes your personal challenge, requiring total dedication, concentration and perseverance.

Now that you have put to practice never saying "I" until asked, high self-esteem talk and magic circle conversations, you have earned the fifth great treasure—Happiness.

Your thoughts are clear and purposeful. It is time to continue your self-esteem odyssey by preparing for the sixth Way To Change—Eliminate Put Downs.

"What you do to others, you do to yourself."

"True knowledge exists in knowing that you know nothing, and in knowing that you know nothing, that makes you the smartest of all."

Chapter 6
Eliminate Put Downs

Low self-esteem people perform daily rituals—low self-esteem rituals. Gossiping, putting people down, dwelling on the past, and constantly complaining are the most popular. Why are these self-destructive activities so popular, such an integral part of society, such a mainstay of the media: radio, television, the Internet, and the movie industry?

Low self-esteem rituals, the *Unacceptables*, give people a sense of superiority—a feeling of **power**. Nasty remarks, body slamming, whining and complaining make low self-esteem sufferers feel good, feel important, feel noticed. Your sixth Way to Change looks at the cause of such self-destructive behavior.

First, people suffering from low self-image get a false sense of "feeling good" and "raising their self-image" by criticizing, contradicting, and making fun of others to the person's face or gossiping behind the person's back.

A low self-esteem person is convinced that, "If I put them down I will bring myself up."

Low self-esteem people are afraid the other person might: (a) be smarter than them, (b) expose them for who they really are, or (c) ridicule and make fun of them.

By putting the other person in their place, the low self-esteem personality feels superior—bigger and better than their opponent. No wonder shock jocks, low self-esteem cartoon characters, and bigot comedians are so popular. Television tabloid talk shows reign supreme. Gossip is gold.

Secondly, low self-esteem people live in the past, dwelling on negative memories or their glory days. You often hear, "If only I was young again!" "I wish I'd known then what I know now!" "I miss the good old days!" "If I'd listened to myself, I wouldn't be where I am today!" One bad memory after the other.

Unfortunately, dwelling on the past causes negative thoughts causing depression, fear, anxiety and stress.

Thirdly, people suffering from low self-esteem have such low opinions of themselves that complaining, whining, and arguing become second nature. People with negative energy complain about their jobs, their paychecks, their marriages, their parents, taxes, the price of groceries, the cost of health insurance, gas prices, the weather—just about everything imaginable.

Question: "What makes low self-esteem people happy?"
The answer: "Nothing!"

Indeed, people with low self-image mistake power and status for true happiness. They are convinced their feelings of power over others by intimidation, verbal threats, bashing, and body slamming—the accumulation of money, materialistic goods, and social status—represents true happiness and success. The more money and power low self-esteem people acquire, the more they desire.

As you will discover, it is not how much money you have, the automobile you drive, or the clothes you wear that matters, it is how you feel about yourself and how others feel about you that really counts.

True power and success comes only from a high self-image.

Happiness is attained through your ability to change your thoughts and a willingness to get along with others. Every individual you meet is your gateway to life-long contentment.

Stop and think. Why would you want to talk about others behind their back, put others down, make fun of people, or hurt their feelings? You only hurt yourself.

SELF PUT DOWNS

Stop putting yourself down. The next time another person compliments you or praises your performance, replying, "Thank you!" will satisfy your self-esteem, your self-worth.

Bashfully mumbling, "Ah, shucks, I can't play piano!" after a great performance, is a sure sign of low self-image. All forms of self-consciousness, shyness, and shame are low self-esteem behaviors you learned as a child.

You were taught it is bad to admit you are pleased with yourself, that you should be ashamed to admit you have self-worth or self-regard. Now that you are aware of your self-esteem rights, you no longer have to put yourself down. Perhaps it is time for a serious self-evaluation, a review of how you treat others, for how you treat others is a direct reflection on how you treat yourself.

It is time to stop wasting energy on negative behavior such as gossiping, bad-mouthing, and ridiculing others. It is time you stop focusing on others and start healing yourself.

LEADERSHIP SKILLS

Below are four leadership skills that will make dramatic improvements in your relationships with others. Practical and proven people skills are:

1. Find The Positives in Others
2. Be a Good Sport
3. Praise Properly
4. Criticize Correctly

1. Find The Positives in Others

When you think, say and believe positive things about others your life changes instantly. Once you master the art of listening, never saying "I", and recognizing others, you discover how to find goodness in others.

The proverb, "If you can't say something nice, don't say anything at all," really works! It is easy to find the good in everyone by reminding yourself they are survivors of low self-esteem childhoods; therefore, they are not to blame for their unacceptable behavior.

You must remind yourself, "It is not their fault."

2. Be A Good Sport

Stop worrying about winning. The next time you play a game of ping pong, chess, trivia or tennis, let the other person win. You quickly become their friend.

When you lose, your opponents love you!

It is not suggested you do not try, or give up, but simply learn to enjoy the game and stop worrying about winning and impressing others with superior play or level of excellence. It is enjoying the competition that counts.

Playing to win simply means do the best you can. When children lose, you must tell them they played well, remind them it is okay to lose, you are proud of their effort.

Too much emphasis is placed on winning in our low self-esteem society. Organized sports is a prime example. The majority of coaches, parents, and sports fans believe winning is not everything—it is the only thing.

This "win at any cost and in your face attitude" is totally unacceptable. It promotes an "obsessed with winning" behavior that carries over into your daily life, behavior that thrives on the "win at all costs" and "annihilate all opposition" lifestyle.

Why? Low self-esteem people with fragile egos cannot stand to lose at anything. Does it really matter who wins any game as long as the game is competitive, as long as you do the best you can? The next time you go to a ball game, or watch a championship game or match on television, relax. It does not matter which team or player wins. It is only a game! Your self-esteem should not depend on your favorite team's performance.

From now on, have fun and do not annihilate and humiliate your opponents in a game of golf, basketball, or tic-tac-toe. Enjoy each and every game for what it is; a good time.

3. Praise Properly

Praise reinforces recognition. When you suffer from low self-esteem you often fail to notice others doing things correctly. You seem to catch people doing the wrong thing, or not doing it your way, or not meeting your expectations. As you learn to stop criticizing and putting others down you learn to be less critical, allowing you to properly recognize, then praise, other people.

What is praise? Praise is proof you are paying attention. Praise is caring about people's actions, accomplishments and focusing on their achievements with direct compliments. Praise follows in the footsteps of recognition, it is offered after good behavior occurs. Praise takes thank you to the next level.

You improve "Thank you!" by saying, "Thank you for the excellent meal, you're a great cook!" or "I could never have finished this project without you!"

Praise provides a positive ending. It is the frosting on recognition's cake. One of life's greatest gifts, praise, is easy to give away and always appreciated.

4. Criticize Correctly

The most challenging communication technique is to constructively criticize an employee, spouse, or child and make them feel good about themselves—maintain their fragile ego. Keep in mind, the more you use high self-esteem leadership, the less you need to use criticism or reprimands in your daily life.

The four-step technique for positive criticism is:

First: Begin In Private With Positive Talk

Always criticize one on one—person to person. Never humiliate someone in front of others. "I'll make them feel so small they'll never do that again" is a low self-esteem technique that surely brings resentment, hard feelings, and isolation. The other person needs to feel you are not attacking their pride or their fragile ego.

Some excellent opening comments are:

"This spread sheet you prepared is very good, however..." or "You've always done the best job possible, I need your opinion on something..." or "I truly appreciate your timely work...I was just noticing..." or "I'm impressed with how hard you've worked on this project, I have an idea I'd like to share with you." or "If you have a moment...I need your help."

Second: Criticize The Behavior, Not The Person

You save a person's feelings by focusing on the problem, not the person. Since it is *how* you criticize that counts, there is the correct way and the incorrect way to criticize.

"Could you run this data base again," is correct. "I don't pay you to make mistakes!" is incorrect.

"I know you will bring your science grade up," is correct. "When I was your age, I got straight A's in biology!" is incorrect.

"This letter is good; however, the introduction needs some revisions," is correct. "You're a terrible writer!" is incorrect.

"Please check these numbers," is correct. "Stupid, any dummy can see the right answer!" is incorrect.

Hear the difference?

Based on, "Don't worry, it was an honest mistake!" as the correct response, here are some low self-esteem criticisms attacking the person's esteem, not the person's behavior. Your emotions are quickly aroused if you think of a child's reaction.

"Of all the stupid mistakes!"

"Can't you do anything right?"

"You will never amount to anything!"

"I give up, you're hopeless!"

"I hate you!"

"You're a total failure, you idiot!"

"How many times do I have to tell you?"

"I'm telling you this for your own good!"

"I wish you were never born!"

These examples remind you that criticizing incorrectly is unacceptable. The next time you reprimand someone, stop and think. Are you criticizing correctly or are you body slamming to belittle them and put them in their place to make yourself feel superior?

Third: End Friendly And Drop It Forever

You must make the other person feel good after discussing their unacceptable behavior. You must boost their dignity, their self-esteem, by letting them know you are on their team. For example, "I know you can do it," or "I'm proud to have you on our staff," or "You have great potential," are all motivational high self-esteem closers. Nevertheless, you often hear:

"Don't ever let me catch you doing that again!"

"Next time, you're fired!"

"I'm watching you mister!"

"Do as I say, not as I do!"

"You'll never learn!"

"I've never met anyone so stupid in my life!"

"Do you have a brain in your head?"

"Nimrod!" Imbecile!"

Again, listen to the incredible difference between the high esteem closers and the low esteem closers.

Fourth: When It's Over, It's Over

You must remember, when an issue is over, it is forgotten. Bury it. Do not dig up dead issues. You can justify calling attention to an error or mistake once. Twice is unacceptable. The third time becomes a nagging put down.

Admit it, dwelling on the past and reminding everyone of their prior mistakes is a major put down to bring yourself up.

Examples of nagging reminders are, "Remember last year when you lost the keys!" or "We'll never forget how you totally embarrassed us when you were growing up!" or "You're going to fail just like last time!" or "Dummy, when will you ever learn?"

Each statement allows the speaker to humiliate the person being reprimanded, an excellent and effective way to gain an unfair psychological advantage. All low self-esteem reminders never help other people do better or improve. Put downs only antagonize and alienate, making things worse.

Letting go of the past, of prior mistakes, and not humiliating the people in your life is a major step on the high road to self-improvement.

SARCASM, JOKING, AND NAME CALLING

Sarcasm, joking, just-kidding remarks, and name calling must be eliminated. Many people grew up with sarcastic parents and teachers who simply did not know any better.

As long as the unwritten code of sarcasm exists, better known as society's "joking and just-kidding rule", people will continue to make fun of each other—do put downs—make racist remarks—all in the good name of "acceptable sarcasm", that is, any excuse to make fun of others.

The truth is, sarcasm, put downs, and making fun of others is a low self-esteem personality trait, one of the *Unacceptables.*

People verbally abuse others and disguise it as a joke or funny incident. After ridiculing and embarrassing another person they laughingly declare, "Just kidding!"

Their victim appears to be smiling or amused, but the person is emotionally hurt, socially upset, and sometimes visibly shaken by the sarcastic statement.

How are they suppose to feel? Their feelings are hurt. Their most prized possession has been attacked—their esteem.

Stand-up comedians, movie stars, and radio celebrities

make racist and bigot remarks about ethnic, religious and social groups, literally the truth about how people feel, and the audience laughs it off as a joke to cover up their own low self-esteem feelings and beliefs—their own deep-seated envy of others. Sarcasm is an excuse to get away with the truth, of how you feel about an issue you are afraid to discuss in serious terms. Sarcasm is your low road to unhappiness.

Take control of your life. Sarcasm, joking, and name calling are serious matters. By now, you are reluctantly admitting, "Criticizing others is one of my favorite past times; it's going to be a hard habit to break."

The next time you make fun of how others look, act or talk, their financial condition, their homes, their furniture, the food they eat, their ethnic backgrounds, religious beliefs, or political preferences; when you envy another person's looks, their personalities, their clothing, automobiles or personal possessions; when you criticize another person's personal views, opinions, and past mistakes, or their careers—stop and think! You are only dragging yourself deeper and deeper into the darkest depths of low self-esteem.

The darkest depths of low self-esteem? "Wait just a minute!" you declare, "Everyone is doing it, why should I be different…I'll end up with no friends, no job, no life!" You might say, "It's so much easier to go along with the crowd, to simply fit in, not make any waves—making fun of others is fun…I like my life the way it is…I like myself the way I am!"

Think. Your thoughts have changed and you know it is too late to turn back to your old lifestyle, your former bad habits.

As you finish your sixth journey, you have traveled too far. You know too much. You have passed the point of no return. Moreover, you are forced to ask yourself some soul-searching questions.

Is your own behavior unacceptable, counter-productive, or undeniably negative? Is your gossiping, ridiculing, and criticizing bringing you down and destroying your personality?

You must admit, is time for a change.

In concluding your sixth Way To Change, certain truths rule your thoughts. Like a slap in the face, you have awakened to self-reality, to the visualization of your own behavior. You realize that the day you stop complaining, stop bad-mouthing and putting down others, stop gossiping and being sarcastic, stop wasting away in the past, and stop being envious of others, is the day you will finally feel good about yourself, experience functional relationships—begin living in bliss.

That time is now. Obtaining the sixth great treasure, Love, presents a critical challenge in your Open Road adventure. It means sweeping away years of bad habits first learned during childhood and reinforced during adulthood.

Prior to beginning your seventh Way To Change—Forgive and Forget—rest and allow your mind the time to reflect on your past behavior.

Think about who you truly are.

"Fulfill the needs of others and all your needs shall be fulfilled. Rather than putting yourself first, put yourself last and you shall end up ahead."

Chapter 7
Forgive and Forget

People with low self-esteem are not capable of forgiveness. They hold grudges. They seldom say they are sorry. They think they are right all the time. Low self-esteem people are full of revenge, hatred, and more often than not, take out their revenge and animosities on everyone around them. Often, you hear someone explain, "Their pride got in the way." or "They're too proud to say they're sorry." Your seventh change begins with the second most misunderstood word in society—pride.

PRIDE

What exactly is pride? The dictionary describes PRIDE as *1. an over-high opinion of oneself b. arrogance, narcissistic. 2. dignity and self-respect.* Interesting. The dictionary gives pride opposite definitions. The first definition perfectly describes low self-esteem, while the second definition describes high self-esteem. The same thing happened with the dictionary's definition of *self-esteem.*

No wonder people become confused trying to understand pride and self-esteem. The reality is, pride is self-esteem and self-esteem is pride. Pride is good. Pride is healthy. People who lack pride suffer from low self-esteem. People with low self-image do not feel proud of themselves or others.

TRUE LOVE

It is time to comprehend the true meaning of the most popular emotional word of all time—love. The following statement will clear up all the confusion in your heart and mind, allowing you to experience the reality of absolute love, of unconditional love—true love.

Only when you have a healthy self-esteem can you experience self-love—only when you love yourself—your Self—can you possibly love another person.

Love is such a wonderful word. The phrase "I love you" sounds so soothing and reassuring as it rolls off your lips. Unfortunately, the word "love" and the phrase "I love you" are the most overused and abused words in most people's day-to-day vocabulary—conversation. As you have already learned, without a healthy self-esteem, true love does not exist. Without self-pride, true love does not exist. Without a high self-image, true love does not exist.

The more high self-esteem you have the more positive your thoughts, and only with positive thinking does the ability to love yourself, your Self, and therefore others, exist.

Stated more simply, only when your self-esteem is healthy do you even like yourself or feel good about yourself. Self-love only exists when you like yourself, when you trust your thoughts, when you respect yourself.

To demonstrate how the word love is misused, an excellent love test is to replace the word love with like, trust, respect, or admire.

In other words, the next time you whisper to someone, "I love you", try replacing the word "love" with "like", "trust", "respect", or "admire" and see how you feel. Are you saying, "I love you," but possibly do not like, trust, or admire the person you are saying it to? Do you unknowingly use low self-esteem love?

LOW SELF-ESTEEM LOVE

It is so easy to confuse low self-esteem love for real love. Low self-esteem love occurs when you have not learned to truly love yourself, but honestly believe you love another person. Once again, your dysfunctional condition, your misconception of love, is not your fault. After all, low self-esteem love is learned in early childhood by observing parents who loved dysfunctionally. Then, is reinforced during adulthood by society in general—especially the media. The media: Internet, books, music, video games, movies, and television portray and promote low self-esteem love every day of your life. You are bombarded with incorrect instructions on how to love, on how to conduct a functional relationship with the people in your life.

THE LANGUAGE OF LOW SELF-ESTEEM LOVERS

Low self-esteem, unfaithful lovers are famous for their "low self-esteem one liners". Unhealthy language between couples with low self-image focuses on feelings of:

• Insecurity: "I'm not good enough!" "Please don't leave me!"
• Selfishness: "I don't care what you think!"
• Jealousy: "I know you look at others when I'm not around!"
• Suicide: "If you leave me, I'll kill myself!"
• Stubbornness: "I'm right; you're wrong!"
• Blame: "You've ruined my life," or "Because of you, I'm overweight and ugly!"
• Conceit: "Aren't I beautiful!" "I hope the children don't end up looking like your side of the family."
• Possessive: "You're mine, all mine!"
• Short-lived: "We've only been married a month and you're already getting on my nerves!"
• Pitiful: "Nobody loves me, poor pitiful me." "I'm ugly!"
• Loneliness: "You don't have to be alone to feel alone."
• Threats: "If you ever leave, I'll take you for all you're worth!"
• Guilt: "Sorry honey, I promise I'll make it up to you."
• Confusion: "You said you'd love me forever, was it only my imagination?"
• Frustration: "I'm tired of games, love's got to be real to me!"
• Co-Dependence: "No one appreciates me, I've been used!"
• Denial: "Wrong? Nothing's wrong!"

Now that you recognize the common language of low self-esteem lovers, you need to understand the reason for their bad behavior, why they act as they do.

LOW SELF-ESTEEM PARTNERS

Low self-esteem love is enacted by people from all walks of life. Many loving relationships are filled with dysfunctional actions and negative behaviors leading to miscommunication, ruined romances, separation, divorce, and single parenthood.

Why?

Low self-esteem partners expect you to make them happy. They love to control you, intimidate you, solve your problems for you, make you behave as they think you should (after all, they know what is best for you), say "yes" when they really mean "no", suffer in loud silence, and make you feel guilty.

Low self-esteem partners love to complain, nag, scream, entrap, accuse, overprotect, stalk, bribe, seduce, play games, provoke, lecture, punish with extended silence, enable, and manipulate.

Partners with unhealthy egos threaten to kill themselves, chase after you, get even with you, dominate you, act helpless, blame their parents, blame their boss, blame society, over eat, over drink, want sex all the time, or not at all, and love to make you jealous. They search your belongings, peek in your wallet, gossip about you, accuse you, physically abuse you, scream they cannot live without you—all in the name of love. Love!

What are the chances of low self-esteem lovers having a functional relationship? Absolutely none. Why? Low self-esteem lovers are insatiably attracted to one another, becoming hopelessly entangled and totally obsessed with their partner, avoiding people who are good for them. Infatuation rules.

Low self-esteem lovers cannot get along—but cannot live without each other. Their daily lives are *dysfunctionally functional*. Relationships between low self-esteem lovers are doomed for failure—unless they change.

HIGH SELF~ESTEEM LOVE

Love is another word for a healthy self-esteem. Love is high self-image. Love is personal pride. Love is attentive listening. Love is never having to say "I" until asked.

Love is many things to many people, but one thing is certain, high self-esteem love is the only love that lasts.

True love is: the ability to love yourself, and therefore, others.

FINDING A SOUL MATE

Selecting your mate for life, a life partner, is a challenge often ending in failure or personal disaster. There are millionaires that would give up their fame and fortune for the right person to spend their life with.

There are multitudes of people worldwide involved in dating services desperately searching for their soul mate, yet divorces and dysfunctional relationships are at an all-time high.

Until you trust yourself, know who you really are, possess more high self-esteem traits than low self-esteem traits, you will select the wrong partner—you will choose poorly.

An openly honest and functional relationship only exists when both partners feel good about themselves, more specifically, when both people in the relationship are continually striving for a high self-esteem existence, a life filled with positive thoughts.

ELIMINATE ANGER

The low self-esteem emotion responsible for creating an unloving, unforgiving, revengeful, jealous and violent lifestyle is anger. Anger is learned during childhood and is perceived by the majority of society as acceptable human behavior.

Acceptable? Well, why wouldn't it be? Anger, often followed by violence, is promoted in all forms of entertainment such as television, movies, the Internet, books, video games, and professional sports.

Anger is everywhere.

Our media heroes teach you that anger is acceptable and the right thing to do, especially when followed with violent acts of revenge. Murder, wife beating, child abuse, and screaming temper tantrums, just to name a few, usually begin in a fit of anger. By controlling anger, the vast majority of violence would never occur. You control the anger in yourself and in others by developing one simple habit: **Never Raise your Voice In Anger!**

During an emotional episode or outburst, a loud voice causes anxiety, tension, stress and anger. Have you noticed how two people get into a shouting match? When one person raises their voice the other person's voice raises (and so on) until both people are using the language of the angry—out-shouting and dominating each other. Violence often follows.

By deliberately keeping your voice soft, it becomes difficult for the other person to begin shouting or to continue screaming. When the other person realizes you are not shouting back, they usually become embarrassed, self-conscious, and immediately calm down.

Your normal voice *forces* the other person to remain calm, thus eliminating rage and self-anger. Screaming at people—chronic yelling—merely announces you suffer from a serious low self-image.

- Screaming parents raise angry, screaming children!
- Screaming teachers produce angry, screaming students!
- Screaming coaches produce screaming players!

When you hold anger in your heart you cannot truly love yourself or the people around you. The next time you feel yourself really losing control, by keeping your voice soft and relaxed you will not become angry or upset. By curbing anger, remaining calm and patient becomes part of your behavior.

Only when you control anger will you experience patience. One day when you least expect it, one magic moment, an incredible calmness will overtake your personality. You will feel relaxed and in total control of your emotions, your voice will remain calm and reassuring.

Controlling, then eliminating anger, is merely your initial step. You must take it to the next level, you must learn to forgive. The key to letting go of rage and anger, letting go of past events, is to forgive and forget.

FORGIVENESS

People with positive thoughts—high self-image—are non-angry and non-violent; thus, they are forgiving. Your life-long forgiveness formula is: **non-anger = forgiveness**. Based on this esteem formula, try a high self-image exercise guaranteed to lift a tremendous emotional burden off your shoulders. Ready?

First, think of all the people you are angry with, mad at, disgusted with, even the people you claim you hate. Be honest, they could be your parents, your spouse, your children, your friends, your relatives, your boss, a coworker, or a complete stranger behind your car in traffic, a "crazy tailgater".

Now, realize that all the people you just thought of suffer from some form of low self-esteem. Since it is not their fault, they learned bad behavior in early childhood and are convinced it is the proper way to behave, how can you be angry with them? It is not their fault. It is time to forgive them, to realize people suffering with the *Emotional Virus* simply cannot help themselves. By forgiving others you immediately acquire a higher self-worth, a calmness, allowing you to get on with your life.

FORGET MEANS LETTING GO

Forgetting low self-esteem traumas in your life is impossible, especially childhood events such as violent or arguing parents, being screamed at, childhood isolation from being ignored, or molestation. But it is possible, as you learn forgiveness, to place bad memories and negative feelings in the back of your mind. In a special place where, every time you remember a bad memory, you go through a forgiveness process—a self-cleansing—allowing your inner-self to deal with the negative thoughts.

In other words, the more forgiving you become, the less you

think or talk about childhood traumas or recent low self-esteem episodes in your life. You learn to let go.

Bad memories become hazier and hazier in your *mind's eye* as you become emotionally healthier and happier with who you are. Self-cleansing is a powerful technique in your search for a healthy self-image.

Rationalize for one moment. Since your parents did not plot and plan to give you low self-esteem (they were childhood victims themselves), you must re-evaluate your feelings for them. It is time to drop all the excess baggage, all the unnecessary pain, all the revenge and anger.

As parents, what about negative feelings you have toward your own children? How can you be upset when you are the one who has given your child low self-esteem in the first place? You have raised your kids just like your parents raised you.

Yes, the legacy of low self-esteem survives deep within your own family, yet, no one is to blame. Blame must be buried.

Change is in the air. You have discovered freedom within by embracing forgiveness. Whether you are thirteen, thirty-three, or ninety-three, you are a potential leader. When you learn forgiveness, you learn leadership.

Soon, everyone around you changes before your very eyes.

The next time you confront a spouse, a parent, a friend, or a supervisor who never listens to you, is never satisfied with your performance, screams to the top of their lungs at you or constantly complains, forgive them.

JEALOUSY

Of all the low self-esteem emotions, perhaps the one emotion that gives you away as an untrustworthy life partner is jealousy.

Jealousy has three ugly children: physical violence, verbal abuse, and hidden agendas.

In romantic relationships, when you are threatened and insecure about the presence of another man or another woman, it is a direct reflection on your self-confidence, your own self-trust. If you do not trust the person you are with, you simply do not trust yourself. When you do not trust yourself, jealousy rules your decisions, wrecks your relationships, ruins your life and undermines your partnerships. Jealousy is one of the *Unacceptables*. Eliminate it or it will destroy you.

BREAK THE CHAIN OF PAIN

Since the legacy of low self-image is passed unknowingly from one generation to the next, low self-esteem family traditions and bad habits form a low self-image cycle or *chain of pain*. That is, each family member is linked together, generation to generation, by a poor self-image kept alive by an unhealthy ego. Because family values are important, you go to great *low self-extremes* to maintain your traditional low self-esteem comfort zone.

Now that you recognize the symptoms of the *Emotional Virus*, it is time to break the chain of emotional pain—to stop low self-esteem dead in its tracks—to make a change in your life and the lives of everyone around you.

EMOTIONAL GROWTH

As you grow emotionally, the people around you change. As you use the high self-esteem techniques that you have learned on your quest for positive energy, as your behavior changes, your life changes forever. You look, act and feel totally different.

As you change and become emotionally healthy, what will everyday life be like? How will the people you live and interact with, especially the family members and friends you have known for years, react to your new behavior—your new personality?

One thing is for certain, positive or negative, there *will* be reactions from everyone around you. You will notice many different social reactions from family members, parents, friends, and coworkers as they observe the change in you. Mixed reactions are disbelief, happiness, suspicion, amazement, anger, confusion, admiration, withdrawal, rejection and jealousy.

Meeting the challenge of negative reactions from friends and loved ones is easier than you think because your commitment to change is stronger than your desire to remain dysfunctional.

Once you discover who you are, there is no stopping your passionate quest for self-improvement.

Here are some examples of what to expect:

"Parents Change"

You have always felt like a failure around your parents; you cannot seem to do anything right. Every conversation is incredibly frustrating, ending in a terrible argument.

Suddenly, by practicing high self-esteem habits, you and your parents get along. Mom and Dad think you act strange because you do not argue or fight with them anymore. You're calm all the time. They even admit they enjoy your company. Your parents cannot believe the change in you.

They are suspicious but seem happily confused. You now get along. You look forward to family functions.

"Peer Group Changes"

Your friends like to gossip and make fun of other people wherever you go. Lately, you have noticed they are uncomfortable around you because you change their awful bad mouthing into positive conversation. You will not condone or become part of their negative fun.

You realize they talk about you behind your back, but as your self-image improves, it does not bother you. Although your friends wonder about you, they secretly respect and admire you. They feel your strength—your emotional power.

"Spouse • Life Partner Changes"

For several years now, you and your spouse, the person of your dreams, have not communicated properly. Lately your spouse realizes you are attentive, listening, and no longer raising your voice in anger.

Your disbelieving sweetheart is so shocked, suspicion has set in. After all, "sweetie" has never seen you act this way before.

Although tentative, your spouse loves the new you. Communication lines have opened up. Your marriage and relationship has never been better.

"Children Change"

Your hyperactive kids have been totally out of control since they were terrible toddlers. Recently, you have changed and stopped yelling and screaming at them and started to listen to every word they say. You are now attentive.

Your emotionally stunned and changing children look at you funny, still flinch when you talk, but you have noticed an immediate and miraculous change in their behavior.

"Teenagers Change"

You always knew little junior would be such a nice boy when he grew up, but when he hit his teens he became your worst nightmare. First, his grades dropped, then the drugs, then the gangs, and finally his total rejection of you—his own parent.

You tried everything, but his bad behavior intensified. Your decision to change allowed you to discover high self-esteem parenting and you have seen dramatic improvement. You no longer get angry and overcritical, and more importantly, you now provide the one thing he wanted most—attention and recognition. Your child is in complete shock with your functional family relationship. The two of you have never gotten along better.

"Employers Change"

You have unsuccessfully managed your office staff like a tyrant since day one. Over the past few years you have hired and fired one employee after the next—no one stays with your company very long. The worst part is, most of the people you hire always end up being predictably unproductive.

Since your recent decision to change—to use high self-esteem management techniques, productivity has increased and your employees are no longer quitting. Some workers are still "gun shy" of you, but they are beginning to trust you. Many of them now look to you for leadership. It has taken several months but the results are incredible.

You look forward to going to the office again. Life is good.

"Strangers Change"

You have always been afraid or nervous to meet new people. Feeling oversensitive, you avoid all strangers, convinced they are "out to get you" and "cannot be trusted". Lately you have tried some magic circle conversation with total strangers and a personal revelation has occurred in your life.

You now realize *why* your career in sales is unsuccessful, *why* you do not seem to fit in at social gatherings, and *why* the people you meet seem unimpressed with you.

You have failed to tap in to your greatest resource—other people. You have finally discovered that the people around you hold the key to your happiness and success. Life has never been more rewarding since your change.

The above examples barely scratch the surface of the real-life dramas that unfold during your quest for high self-esteem.

What will be your most challenging situation—your most frustrating experience?

Patience. The longer you have known someone, the longer it will take to convince them you are actually changing—becoming a better person. But with self-patience, time becomes your welcomed friend.

HIGH SELF-ESTEEM HEROES

As a child, your first heroes were your parents, stepparents, grandparents and guardians. Soon teachers became your heroes in school, and eventually, you idealized and worshiped media heroes. Movie and television stars, rock stars, sports figures, radio celebrities, authors, politicians, and the wealthy have become your new heroes.

You have been taught to idealize and worship the rich and famous, for they represent your hopes and dreams.

However, your quest has uncovered a critical clue in solving the mystery of self-esteem. People suffering from low self-image seek constant attention and recognition, craving the spotlight of life.

Perhaps you should evaluate your heroes prior to using them as positive role models, prior to emulating their behavior, prior to wanting to be like them. After all, your heroes might suffer from the *Emotional Virus*.

Life's journey is full of emotional traps and misleading paths. Beware. Selecting the wrong role models is a life-long mistake.

Seek people with positive energy as your heroes.

In concluding your seventh Way To Change, you realize that the combination of pride, love, non-anger, and forgiveness make you the person of your dreams, the person you have always wanted to be. For the first time in your life, you calmly and confidently deal with all conflicts, all challenges, and all changes in your daily life. There are many.

Your ability to forgive and forget, to love yourself and the people around you, to control your anger and possess high self-esteem passion, rewards you with the seventh great treasure—Knowledge.

An incredible transformation has occurred in your life as you enter the final passage of your inspirational journey—the eighth Way To Change—Live Life as a Leader.

"One must have chaos in oneself to give birth to a dancing star."

Chapter 8
Live Life As A Leader

Nothing happens by accident. Your arrival here, reading these words, has happened at the perfect time. When this esteem experience comes to a finish, you shall know it absolutely. All the messages in this book have arrived in your life at just the right time—now.

THE POWER OF NOW

Change begins right now. "Now" means at this very moment. Not tomorrow or at some future date. You must learn to live in the moment. You will know this magic feeling when you stop worrying about past things and future events, when you stop being attached to outcomes.

Simply focus on the task at hand, this moment. Just be. There is no time but this time, this moment. There is nothing else to think about but now. The past and the future are merely illusions within your mind. They exist because you create them in your imagination.

You imagine the past and future, but they do not exist outside the now. Nothing, no thing, exists outside this present moment. The choice is yours, you may either seize the moment, *"carpe diem"*, or focus your thoughts somewhere else and suffer the consequences.

Instead of living in the present moment, you often choose to live in the past, or spend your time dreaming of your future. Your life is spent anxiously waiting for that right time to make something happen—some *thing* that will supposedly bring you instant happiness.

Then, you never obtain happiness when the future does finally arrive. Why? Because happiness is only available right here, right now, in this exact moment.

You ask yourself, "Where did my life go?" "Where did the time go?" You fail to realize that you spent all of your time dreaming about your future, or, even worse, thinking negative thoughts about your past—living in the past.

Remember, a tree grows from a seedling. A tower starts with one brick. A journey of a thousand miles begins with a single step. Enormous projects seem small when you begin small, one step at a time.

Whatever the task, simply begin from right here, right now. Everything is possible from here because now is all there is. Do not worry about the result.

There is always a new journey awaiting you. There is a time for everything. To everything, turn, turn, turn. Just as you breathe in and breathe out, there is a time to be ahead and a time for being behind, a time for being in motion and a time for being at rest, a time for being vigorous and time for being exhausted, and a time for being safe and a time for being in danger.

Live in the moment and free yourself from the chase.

Stop striving for more and searching for something better. You already have everything you need to be completely happy, right here, right now.

There is no time, only the eternal moment of now.

- **The Past Is History**

- **The Future Is Unknown**

- **All You Have Is Right Now**

- **Live In The Moment**

- **Be Happy ... Now!**

NOTHING, NO THING, CAN MAKE YOU HAPPY

Nothing, no thing, can make you happy. For instance, think of your birthday presents. Remember when you were a child, waiting days and weeks in anticipation of that special birthday gift? You believed that your birthday surprise would make you happy forever.

Did it?

As you grew older, you believed other things or events would bring you years of happiness. Things such as:

- Finding that special person.
- Earning more money.
- Buying that new car.
- Purchasing clothes and jewelry and more stuff.

If you think about it, none of these things ever made you happy for more than a few hours, days, or weeks. The reality is:

There is no way to happiness, happiness *is* the way.

Another way of living happily is:

- Do not ACT ... Simply BE.
- Do not ACT happy ... BE happy.
- Do not ACT honest ... BE honest.
- Do not ACT forgiving ... BE forgiving.
- Do not ACT loving ... BE loving.

The key to personal freedom is realizing that nothing, no thing, can make you happy—happiness *is* the way.

PERSONAL FREEDOM

"I come first" or "I'm number one" sounds so selfish and self-centered. You hear such negative opinions about the "me generation" or the "looking out for number one" philosophy.

Why?

Because "I come first" originates from low self-esteem behaviors, and as you have learned thus far, people with the *Emotional Virus* ruin society by thinking only of themselves and no one else.

It is time for an attitude adjustment, a change of heart.

In your quest for personal freedom, "I come first" actually means feed your esteem, take care of your emotional needs, celebrate your liberation from low self-image—negative thinking.

When you take care of your self-worth, you no longer tolerate harassment. You will not succumb to threats or terrorism. Violence has no place in your life. All forms of unacceptable behavior are dealt with in a quick, decisive and confident manner. You will discontinue your relationships with people who choose to harm or harass us.

You now refuse to let anyone upset your stable lifestyle, or interfere with your self-success and happiness. You are now in total control of your life. You know who you are.

No matter how traumatic the times or the events, you live with inner-peace and tranquility. When you come first, that is, when you beam with high self-esteem, you let the good thoughts and memories in, keeping the bad thoughts and memories out.

You let the good people in, keeping the bad people out. You are in emotional control of your life. You have found personal freedom—freedom within.

NOTHING OCCURS IN YOUR LIFE THAT IS NOT FIRST A THOUGHT

Nothing occurs in your life, no thing, which is not first a thought. Thoughts are your life magnets, drawing positive or negative effects to you. Your thoughts never die, even when you cease to be.

When a thought, good or bad, crosses your mind, it creates vibrations that travel around the world and out into the universe.

Thoughts travel faster than light—infinite speed, entering the minds of others and producing similar thoughts.

A person with hateful, jealous or violent thoughts sends out those negative vibrations, which in turn, enter the minds of millions of other people, stirring up the same negative thoughts.

Good thoughts help others, bad thoughts harm others. It is that simple.

When your thoughts are noble, loving thoughts, their vibrations enter all sympathetic minds. They send out similar thought vibrations, resulting in pure love.

Thoughts create this world, your world, every world. Thought brings everything, every thing, into existence.

Thoughts are like objects. Just as you can hand another person an apple, you can also hand them your powerful thoughts.

Thoughts pass between and among all persons. A person of powerful thoughts can influence a person of weak thoughts. When you learn to control your thoughts, you will become as one with a Supreme Being—The Source, and the universe.

As the greatest force in the universe, thoughts are the most powerful weapon in your personal *armor*.

This is why you must be careful with your thoughts. Every thought you think always comes back to you. If you send hateful thoughts, hate will come back to you. When you think and send loving thoughts, love will come back to you.

You get what you think about, whether you want it or not. Whether your thoughts are negative or positive, they always come true.

Your thoughts manifest your destiny. Think you are worthless, worthless you will become. Think you are ugly, ugly you will become. Think you are patient, patient you will become. Think you are loving, loving you will become.

Now that you know the powerful effect of thoughts on your life, and that most of your thoughts are negative, you must learn to STOP and think again.

STOP! AND THINK AGAIN

The way to stop your negative thoughts, your *stinking thinking*, is to catch yourself thinking a negative thought.

During your internal conversations, when you talk to yourself and hear yourself think a negative thought, STOP and immediately think to yourself, "I'm not like that," or "That's not like me." Then, immediately exchange the bad thought for a positive one.

Your life changes that instant. Changing your thoughts changes your life.

Learn to say, "Stop! That's not like me!" "Stop thinking like that!" "I know better!"

Then, change your thoughts to a positive one. The most effective, life-changing positive thoughts are affirmations.

THE POWER OF AFFIRMATIONS

Affirmations are a statement of fact that you say to yourself, silently or out loud. Affirmations are positive statements, often written down so you can remember them.

Affirmations are never something you want or wish for.

It is you asserting the truth about something.

You cannot *want* the statement to be true. Your statement must be something you already know to be true!

Do not think "I want," think "I *have!*" Rethink "I want happiness," to "I *have* happiness!" Do not want, choose! You will be shocked at how quickly your life changes for the better. Affirming is a three step process:

1. Affirm Your Thoughts:
- Put your affirmations in writing.
- Your affirmations are for you, not for others.
- When stating affirmations, use action words: visualize the event and the positive outcome.
- Be realistic with your affirmations.
- Share your affirmations with positive people, not negative thinkers who will question you, criticize you, and try to convince you that you are not worthy of your affirmation.

2. **Reaffirm to make sure your thoughts are positive and never contain negative statements:**
   - Examples of affirmative beginnings:
     "I am _____!"
     "I have _____!"
     "I always _____!"
     "I take pride in _____!"
   - Avoid saying:
     "I want to _____!"
     "I'll never _____!"   "I will not _____!"
     "I'm going to stop drinking when _____!"

Affirmations are:

"I am in control of my life."
"My life is in order."
"I am happy."
"People and events come into my life at just the right time."
"I am a loving, worthwhile person."
"I am logical and decisive in making decisions."
"I am honest."
"I feel good I left drugs and alcohol behind."
"I take great pride in living clean and sober."
"I enjoy friends with similar values."
"My present thoughts determine my future."
"I treat all people with dignity and respect."
"I am a good person."
"I look for and enjoy new challenges."
"I feel relaxed and confident."
"I take pride in being organized."
"I enjoy listening to others."
"It is easy for me to control my emotions. I am calm and patient."
"Every day I make progress."
"I deserve happiness and success."
"I enjoy affirmations and positive results."

3. Live Your Daily Affirmations:
- Write down you affirmations.
- Read your affirmations daily.
- Visualize your positive thoughts.
- Feel your affirmations passionately. Your vision must be emotionally charged with extreme passion.
- Affirmations are thoughts; therefore, thoughts are messages to the universe/God!
- Thinking, "It is my intention to _____, is a vibrational message to the universe/God!

POSITIVE THINKING

Until you acquire enlightenment, the first thoughts that enter your mind are usually negative. You hear people say, "My mind is in a rut." Be patient. Change does not happen instantly. Until you learn to stop thinking like that, there is another method besides affirmations that will help you change.

Close your eyes and think of your favorite thing to do.

Now, think of that word again as the first thought that enters your mind.

How do you feel when you hear that word?

Your most likely answer is, "Happy!" Now, close your eyes and see the <u>action</u> of the word in your mind's eye.

Visualize your thoughts.

How do you feel? Positive? This is because your mind, every cell in your body, is enjoying the release of positive chemicals. When your first thought is negative, simply change that thought to something positive that you can visualize and feel.

You must learn to change your negative thinking—STOP thinking like that. Right now, close your eyes and think of something negative that truly bothers you. Now, think the exact opposite thought. A happy thought. Think of your favorite song. Do you feel that positive energy? Do you feel the happiness flowing through you?

The grand feeling you have right now must be remembered

and reenacted in your mind over and over again until it becomes part of you. These grand thoughts are manifestations to the universe/God. By visualizing positive feelings in your mind, as well as learning to use affirmations, you have learned that your thoughts *do* control your emotions. Once your thoughts become more positive, there is something else you will learn. Action. You must **act** your thoughts out. Action is required, not just thoughts. The words are not enough. You must do something about your positive thoughts.

Thinking compassionate thoughts are wonderful, but until you treat someone compassionately, your thoughts are nothing but ideas, good ideas, but not yet reality. You must experience the act of compassion to be truly compassionate.

Words themselves are ineffective. Do not just think loving and generous thoughts, *be* loving and generous.

YOU BECOME WHAT YOU THINK ABOUT

Thoughts are like magnets, drawing effects to you. Therefore, when you say to yourself: "I'm not worthy," or "I'm a loser" or "I'm cursed, nothing ever goes my way," these negative thoughts bringing negative results.

In other words, you manifest that which you think about most. You become what you think about. Thinking of your past mistakes guarantees that you will manifest them in the future. This is because you *see* yourself as you think you are.

Your thoughts determine your experience. Think positive thoughts—visualize your positive thoughts, and your brain will make sure that is what you see. People have learned this message from sages for centuries: "You become what you think about," and "You are your thoughts."

The Law Of Attraction guarantees that you get what you think about, whether you want it or not. Thoughts are the basis for the Law Of Attraction. Simply stated, thoughts have an energy that attracts like energy. These energized thoughts release pheromones of measurable energy.

This means that energy matches up with similar energy. When you surround yourself with negative-thinking people, you will share their negative thoughts. This of course, leads to negative events—unhappiness.

(-) Negative thoughts attract low energy vibrations and negative responses in your life.

(+) Positive thoughts attract high energy vibrations and positive responses in your life.

Thought energy, if there is enough of it, forms a shared reality known as **collective consciousness**. When people share the same like thoughts astonishing things happen.

When love is the like thought, miracles happen. When individuals or societies live in fear, astonishingly negative things happen.

EMOTIONAL HEALTH

You suffer emotionally and physically because the low self-esteem *Emotional Viruses* has infected your mind—your fragile esteem. Although born from perfection, your youthful thoughts have been altered by your parents, teachers, politicians and leaders—all of them infected with the *Emotional Virus*. You are made to believe everything but the truth.

You are taught to never think for yourself, to never trust your own thoughts. Thought waves are extremely contagious.

The prime example is the pandemic *Dark Essence*, Earth's on-going epidemic—the *Low Self-Esteem Thought Viruses*.

Low self-esteem is highly contagious, like an emotional cancer. When you think a negative thought of anger or revenge or jealousy, you produce a similar thought in those who surround you.

Your moods infect others. Your diseased, low-self-image thoughts leave your mind and they enter the minds of the people nearest you; then, the minds of others far away, on the other side of the world, on the other side of the universe.

Positive, cheerful thoughts within your mind work the same

way, producing positive thoughts in others. Good thoughts are extremely contagious, traveling great distances. When you suffer from low self-image, when you lack enlightenment, there is a constant battle in your mind between two hungry wolves, a good wolf and a bad wolf. Do you know which wolf wins this battle in your mind? The wolf you feed.

Good and bad do not exist in the universe. Your imagination makes it so. Your mind creates the world of good and bad, happy or unhappy, according to your own thoughts. In other words, nothing can make you happy, happiness *is* the way. Your mind, your total intelligence, exists within each of the millions of cells throughout your entire body.

INTELLIGENT CELLS

Every cell in your body is endowed with intelligence. Every thought you have is conveyed directly to your cells, reacting to your present state of mind. When you are confused or depressed, your thoughts transmit a negative message throughout your nervous system to every cell in your body.

Next, your cells become weak; they can no longer function properly. You soon suffer from physical weakness and diseases. Your intelligent cells, experiencing unhappiness and hopelessness, produce inharmonious vibrations. The mind of each intelligent cell fills with fear and anxiety.

If just one thought cell in your brain becomes infected with the emotional cancer, it spreads to all the other thought cells and eventually your entire thought process is destroyed. You die emotionally. Your cancerous emotions eventually kill your physical body.

Mental health is more important than physical health.

Your body produces powerful chemicals based on thoughts alone. Your glands secrete chemical messages. All your body's hormones determine your emotional health and happiness.

Positive thoughts cause your mind to release positive chemicals, resulting in happiness—bliss.

It is a self-esteem cycle, positive thoughts to positive chemicals to happiness. Happiness produces more positive thoughts and the cycle continues, over and over again.

A happy mind results in a happy and healthy body.

Unfortunately, unhappiness rules the thoughts of most people. Negative thinking causes negative chemicals—toxins that attack the body resulting in unhappiness.

Unhappiness results in more negative thinking—an endless cycle of misery, depression and emotional illness. Physical illness is also a result of negative thoughts.

When you have a happy mind, you have a happy body. A healthy mind promotes a healthy body. All your illnesses and depressions and anxieties and fears come from negative thinking.

Keep in mind, stress does not exist in the universe, only you thinking stressful thoughts!

All negative thoughts form a triad of negative energy.

First, they harm the thinker. Secondly, they harm the person(s) being thought about. Third, they harm everyone by filling the ethereal realm, the air between all humans, with negative energy. A triple curse.

When you radiate thoughts of revenge, you injure the person to whom you direct the hateful thoughts. It is, in fact, your own suicide, for the revengeful thoughts come back to destroy you. As the wise motto states, "What goes around, comes around."

ENJOY ALL THINGS, NEED NOTHING

You need nothing. No thing. Stop needing. Stop wanting. By not wanting, all things will fall in their proper place. When you stop needing, you become calm and free from want. Inner freedom brings inner peace, the ultimate experience. When you live with inner peace, you discover you can live without. Things from the outside world become unimportant. You will experience personal freedom. Freedom within.

Eliminate fear. Stop being afraid of everything. When you eliminate fear, you eliminate anger. Anger is the curse of mankind. When you stop needing things, you become free from fear and anger.

Stop needing physical and emotional gratification. You need nothing from others.

Think. You came from nothing. Nothingness. No-thing-ness.

You came from a place of no things and you will return to a place of no things. You need nothing, yet, you may enjoy all things—all that stuff you collect and believe to be so important. You know, those worldly possessions you covet and fight over and kill each other for.

You believe your accumulation of things will bring you happiness and success. The more you get, the more you desire. It does not take long before you suffer from the disease of more and lose touch with yourself, your center.

Other than the basic necessities of life—food, shelter and clothing, what do you really need? The stuff you accumulate cannot bring happiness. When you glorify wealth, power and beauty, you beget crime, envy, and shame.

Do the things you buy yourself bring everlasting joy?

Always needing *things* becomes an obsession. You become fearful of not getting them; therefore, you become anxious and angry. You are taught that things, possessions, make you happy. When you do not get them, you sulk and become angry.

Do not reject all pleasures of the mind and body. All things of the body must be voluntary, not mandatory.

Do not be a slave to things because you feel you must have them. If you choose to have materialistic goods, so be it. Just remember, inner peace frees you of outside needs.

This inner freedom allows you to love unconditionally.

When you stop needing and wanting things, you will be happier. One day you will know when enough is enough. When you realize you have enough, you are truly rich. The less you desire, the better you feel.

Need nothing.

Embrace this Universal Truth and you will live a long life. When you discover the Great Way, you will surely live forever.

THERE ARE NO ACCIDENTS IN THE UNIVERSE

No accidents occur in the universe. Things do not just happen randomly, or by God's intervention. The supreme reality is that observation, thoughts and beliefs, cause energy waves to take shape. Energy waves turn into particles based on the individual thoughts and beliefs of the observer.

"What observer?" you ask.

Anyone. Any person may observe. You are an observer. Your friends are observers. Everyone is an observer. Energy waves act and respond to your thoughts and beliefs at the moment of observation. This supreme truth brings you right back to the power of thought.

Your thoughts are also creative. When observing, your thought energy directly transmutes wave forms into subatomic particles which, in turn, take form in proportion to what you, the observer, believe. Thoughts take on physical form based on the perception of the thinker. Energy does not need to travel through space and time to communicate, it is already interconnected with all the other energy in the entire universe!

All things in the infinite universe, the entire cosmos, are interconnected. Everything is a galactic vibrating ball of infinite energy communicating with no regard for space and time, traveling at infinite speed. When this energy joins together it forms one, individual thought. One.

The vibrational communication between energy waves happens at precisely the same time, instantly, no matter how far away they are from each other, anywhere in the cosmos. The cells of your body, your DNA, reacts to your thoughts.

Energy waves do not need to travel, they are interconnected to all other energy in the vast universe. A matrix, a vibrational grid of energy, exists throughout the cosmos. Your thoughts and beliefs and intuitions regarding all the events of your life, the way you think, determines exactly how your life will unfold in your physical world. Thought waves of energy have everything to do with your health, happiness and success.

YOU ARE NOT A VICTIM OF CIRCUMSTANCE

You are not a victim of circumstance. You are the creator of your own reality. Your thoughts are determined by your beliefs. You broadcast these thought waves out into the infinite matrix of energy like a radio transmitter.

Your thought waves are transformed from the spiritual realm, the invisible, into particles of the visible, material realm. These join with similar energy waves that all vibrate at the same harmonious frequency and collectively join, unite. This union is what you come to see, feel and experience in its pure physical form as your physical world. You create and shape your own life. No one else does it but you. You and your thoughts.

By controlling your thoughts, you create you world. You create your destiny.

An object cannot exist independently of its observer. The act of observing an object, or an event, or a condition, or a circumstance, causes it to be there. All outcomes are based on your decisions, your choices, and how you observe it.

What you think about an object, event, or circumstance—anything, and believe it to be true, determines your life path. The real truth or the perceived reality does not matter. All that matters is what you think and believe to be true.

If you believe that love is hard to come by, consciously or subconsciously, this projected thought energy is transmitted, broadcast and harmonizes with similar thought waves. These transmute into particles that attract like particles, like attracts like, and your belief that "love is hard to come by" will materialize into absolute truth.

It works the same with money, or health, or a career, or anything you believe in. As you think and believe, so will your life unfold in perfect order.

THE POWER OF CHANGE

Your esteem is your perception of yourself, what you think about yourself. How you feel about your Self is your most important reality. Your self-image is either positive—high self-esteem, or negative—low self-esteem. One or the other dominates your personality within your mind, your unique World of Self.

When you have high-frequency thought vibrations, you enjoy high self-esteem. This is because the fast-moving energy vibrations create your highest thoughts.

When your thought vibrations are low frequency, slow-moving energy, you suffer from low self-esteem. This is because your thoughts vibrate at a low level—slowly.

These slow vibrations produce negative thoughts. Your negative thinking is a direct result of the *Emotional Virus—Dark Essence*, the low self-esteem disease. The destructive viral epidemic has infected human beings for the past 50,000 years. Since the dawn of social awareness, humans have been plagued by a crippling emotional disease that has infected their thoughts.

Times are changing. A self-esteem revolution is upon us. A new world order has appeared on the bright horizon.

In the next few decades you will observe entire generations not passing the dreaded *Emotional Virus*—low self-esteem—on to their children.

Society will begin the long-awaited miracle of healing itself emotionally as all humans recognize themselves and each other for who they are: loving individuals equal in all things.

The eventual elimination of all low-esteem personalities will produce a hitherto unknown society—a peaceful world where everyone gets along—a collective consciousness of functional behavior—a universal, loving World of Self.

In concluding your eighth change, your eighth Way To Change, you have discovered two sides to life: the high self-esteem side and the low self-esteem side.

Every action you take is based on your self-image, either high self-image or low self-image. As you continue your search for self-improvement—freedom within—your understanding of who you can be cleanses your shame and confusion, eliminating all your self-doubt, all your negative thoughts.

Before this experience, you lived your life in darkness and fear. Having emerged from the darkness, you now embrace the light. You see the truth in all things. You have found your self—who you truly are.

You no longer recognize your former life, your previous way of thinking. You have discovered who you are, the path to happiness.

Remain at peace with yourself and do not allow low energy people to affect you in anyway. Remember, you have no enemies; specifically, those who suffer from the *Emotional Virus*—low self-esteem. Forgive them; they have no idea of what they are doing. They have not experienced the epiphany of esteem. They have not changed their thoughts.

Now that *you* have been enlightened, you know how to change your thoughts, and therefore, others.

You are now a leader. With calm words and actions, with confident humility, you may speak grandly so that others feel your love and wisdom, so they follow you on the high road.

Change the way things are.

Become a champion of change. Make a difference by seeking the highest truth. Live life as a leader.

You now understand exactly what the motto: "Live Life as a Leader" means. You have broken free from your chains of pain, from your shackles of guilt and negative thinking.

You are now, at this very moment, free. Free to live life's ultimate rewards—the treasures of self-realization, self-actualization, and a high self-image—to know who you are.

You are no longer afraid. You no longer suffer from fear of others, from fear of yourself, from fear of your own decisions, or even the fear of death.

You have rewritten your life script and you feel a self-transformation—a life-changing epiphany.

By practicing change, you now understand others. By understanding others you now understand your Self. By understanding your Self you now understand the universe.

When you understand others you acquire knowledge. When you understand yourself, your Self, you acquire wisdom.

The eighth Way To Change has shown you the high road—The Great Way—the path to personal freedom—freedom within.

The eighth great treasure—Wisdom—is now yours.

Now go and live the highest truth.

*"There is no greater misfortune
than wanting, always wanting more.
There is no greater curse than discontentment.
Contentment alone is enough.
Indeed, the bliss of eternity may be
found in your contentment."*

More books, novels, and maps by
Mel Wayne

MILLENNIUM ADVENTURES

- Esteem: Discover Who You Are -
(Illustrated Deluxe Edition)
- Hunter Wainright: The Way -
- Atlas of Millennium -
- The Great Way: 81 Oracles -
- Heroes From Earth -
- Girl In Two Worlds -
- Morph: Sage of the Ages -
- Morphisms: Quotations of the Ages -
- Millennium Maps -
- Millennium Videos -

Hunter Wainright: The Way
B&W, Deluxe Edition, Ebook

Hunter Wainright: The Way, is a philosophical adventure novel featuring the characters, maps and landscapes of the planet Millennium. The soft-cover, 6" x 9", has 488 pages. The illustrated, full color, 8.5" x 11", deluxe edition contains 364 pages.

Atlas of Millennium

Atlas of Millennium depicts more than 3,548 mythological names shown on full-color physical, political, and parchment maps, including characters and landscape scenes of Millennium. Illustrated, 8.5" x 11", full color with 224 pages. Includes index.

Heroes From Earth
Book One: Nemoria

Heroes From Earth - Book One: Nemoria is an Role Play Game book featuring the story world of Millennium in a fusion of pen and paper with modern game master aids featuring videos and grid maps. Illustrated, full color, 8.5" x 11", with 128 pages.

Girl in Two Worlds
B&W, Deluxe Edition, Ebook

Written as a companion book to *Hunter Wainright: The Way* by Mel's creative partner, Pamela Wayne, this adventure novel tells the story of Julia Wainright on the same time line as Hunter. Illustrated, full color deluxe edition, 8.5" x 11", with 208 pages.

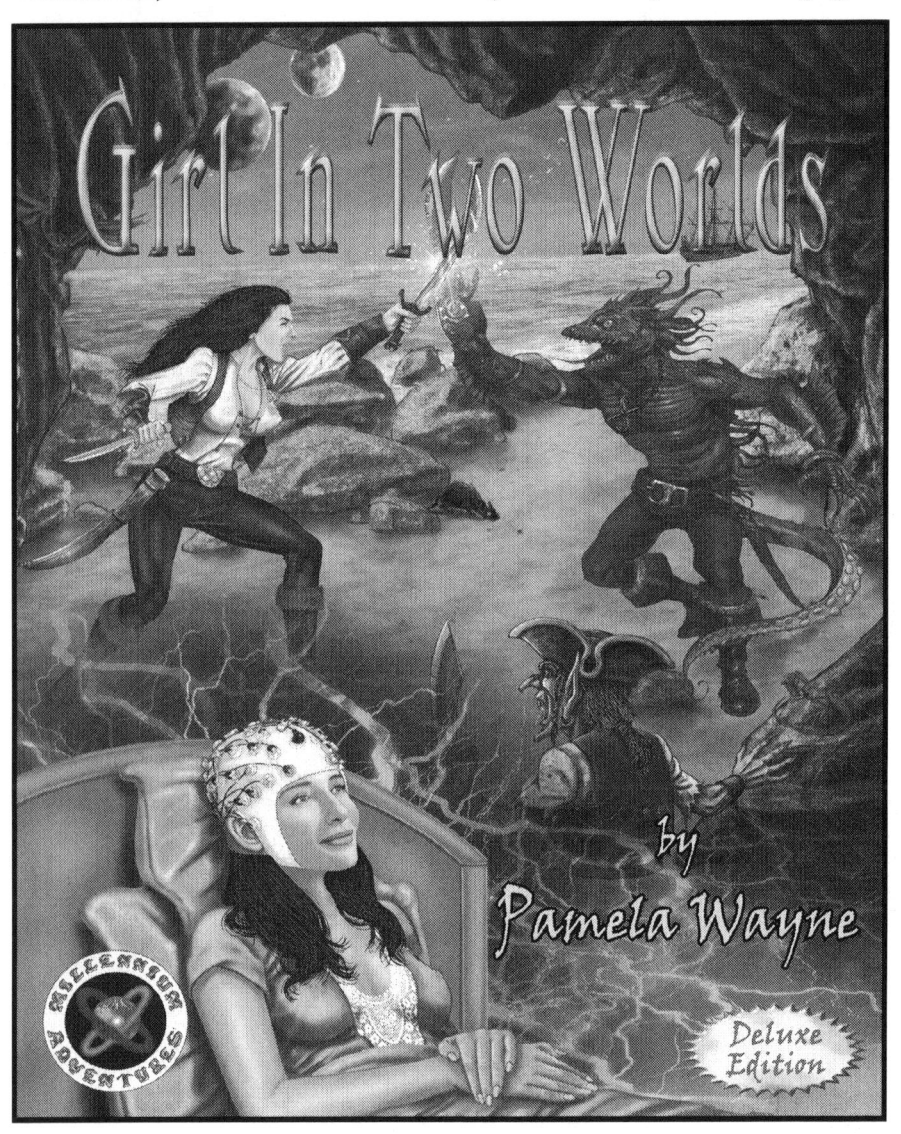

The Great Way: 81 Oracles

The Great Way: 81 Oracles, told by Metamorphosis, Sage of the Ages, unlocks the ancient mysteries of his 81 oracles. Offered as an illustrated Ebook, 6" x 9" black and white edition, and the illustrated, full-color, 8.5" x 11" deluxe edition with 224 pages.

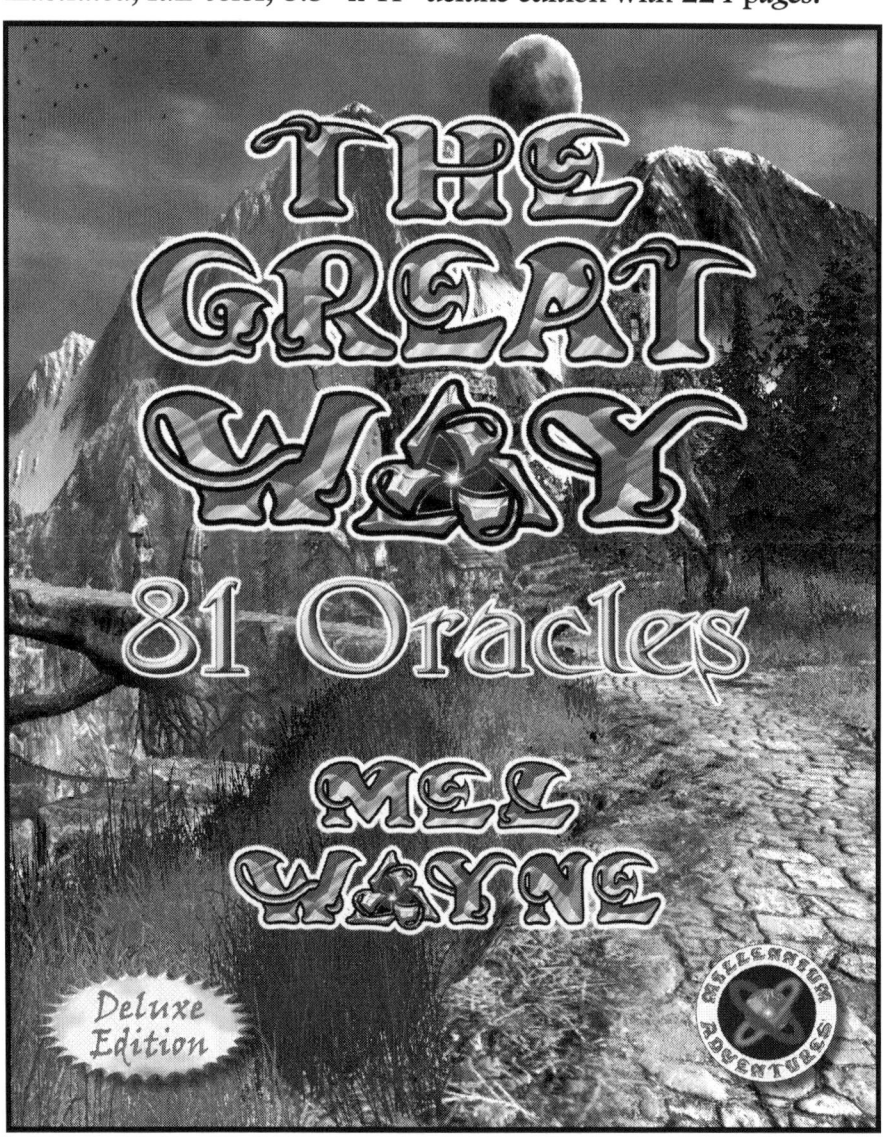

Morph
Sage of the Ages

Morph, Sage of the Ages, reveals the Secrets of the Universe—the Universal Truths—inspiring you to discover who you really are. Features Millennium characters, landscapes, and maps in the illustrated, full color, 8.5" x 11" book with 144 pages.

Morphisms
Quotations of the Ages

Metamorphosis, Sage of the Ages, reveals his words of wisdom that he bestowed upon the most notable philosophers, sages, and Masters of human history. Socrates, Plato, Aristotle, Lao Tzu, Homer, Aesop, Dante, Descartes, Shakespeare, and so many more who visited the great sage, brought back his universal wisdom—inspirational messages—to share with us. Illustrated, full color, 8.25" X 6" book with 212 pages.

Millennium Maps
Upperworld & Underworld

The Upperworld and Underworld Maps of Millennium reveal more than 3,548 mythological names and places, story book lands, legends, fairy tales, and folklore. Color, 24" x 32" size.

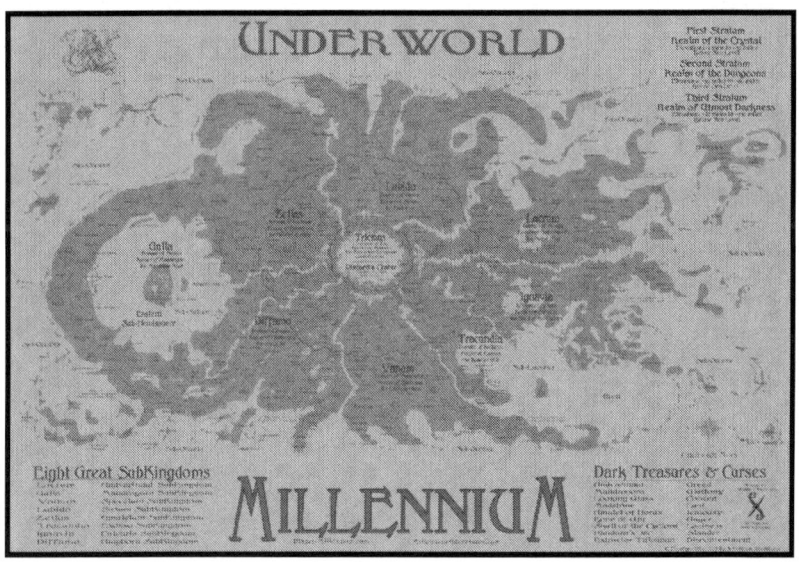

Millennium Videos
Six Landscape Realms

The videos reveal the surreal landscapes of five realms of Millennium: Time Island, Fog Harbor, Dungeon of Fire, Bridge of Riddles, and the Cosmic Cave, plus an introductory video.

- Video 1: Enoch Chronicles
- Video 2: Time Island
- Video 3: Fog Harbor
- Video 4: Dungeon of Fire
- Video 5: Bridge of Riddles
- Video 6: Cosmic Cave

"If you seek to understand the universe,
you shall understand nothing.
If you seek only to understand your Self,
you shall understand the whole universe."

Printed in Great Britain
by Amazon